Mr. Dennis C. Dickerson

# DEFENDER

# OF THE RACE

## James Theodore Holly
## Black
## Nationalist
## Bishop

David M. Dean

Lambeth Press
Boston, Mass

Library of Congress Cataloging in Publication Data
Dean, David M.
Defender of the race
Bibliography: p. 132
1. Holly, James Theodore, 1829–1911.
2. Eglise Orthodox Apostolique Haitienne—Bishops—Biography.
3. Bishops—Haiti—Biography.      I. Title.
BX5999.5.Z8H643   283'.092'4   [B]   78-26913
ISBN 0-931186-02-1

For Martha

# Contents

# Acknowledgments

This book is the product of many hands. I would like to express my appreciation to all those who rendered aid and encouragement. I am particularly grateful to Nelle Bellamy, archivist, friend, and former employer, for the unrestricted use of the Archives and Historical Collections—Episcopal Church (formerly the Church Historical Society), and to Barnes F. Lathrop, who with unbelievable diligence and patience directed the dissertation that grew into this book. I also wish to thank Harold Booher for the use of an office in the library of the Episcopal Theological Seminary of the Southwest. I must acknowledge the helpful cooperation of the staffs of St. Luke's Church, New Haven; The Episcopal Diocese of Connecticut Archives, Trinity College; the Maryland Diocesan Archives, Maryland Historical Society; the Lambeth Library and the United Society for the Propagation of the Gospel, London; the Fisk University Library; the Moreland Collection of Howard University; the Schomburg Collection of the New York Public Library; the Buffalo (New York) Historical Society; the Manuscript Division of the Library of Congress; the National Archives; the Boston Public Library; the New York Public Library; the Sterling and Beinecke Libraries, Yale University; and the interlibrary loan departments of the University of Texas at Austin and Frostburg State College.

I am grateful to Floyd John Miller and Roscoe Pierson for sharing their materials with me; to Howard Miller, Jack Sunder, and John Wiseman for their suggestions and criticisms of the manuscript; to my sister Sarah for helping in the research; to Shelley Drees for typing the final draft; to Richard Newman of Lambeth Press for seeing Holly into print; and to my wife Martha Dean, whose unflagging energy and sharp editorial eye contributed greatly to this book.

June 1978

**I**       

The 100,000 free Negroes living in the antebellum North found themselves in a hostile environment. Their class represented the bottom rung of free society. Collective white prejudice victimized the Northern Negro. He was allowed to possess neither the power nor status necessary for individual dignity, pride, and respect. Medical science labeled him "inferior," and his short life span was spent warding off ever-present poverty. He was seated in a special section of the church, segregated into separate schools, and usually denied admittance to public restaurants, lectures, and transportation. In death his corpse was relegated to a remote corner of a potter's field. This was the society that welcomed James Theodore Holly into the world on October 3, 1829.[1]

## I

The Hollys had been free since 1772, when a Scotsman, James Theodore Holly, the master and father of a Maryland slave, manumitted his namesake son. Reuben Holly, the son of freedman James Theodore Holly, married the recently freed mulatto daughter of an Irish Catholic named Butler, and in 1799 moved his family to the infant capital of the United States.[2]

Racial antagonism in the burgeoning District of Columbia was evidenced by vocal ridicule and petty harassment. It was possible, however, for the free Negro to find work. Many partly erected residences and incomplete public buildings dotted the landscape. Obviously laborers, regardless of skin color, were needed for building projects. Although hired slaves assumed much of the burden of manual labor and consequently lowered the wages of free laborers, Reuben Holly easily found work on the construction of the Capitol. Congress worked only after the harvest season and before the spring planting, but Holly's employment was steady. By 1800, when the federal government officially set up housekeeping in Washington City, 123 of the city's 3,200 inhabitants were free blacks.[3]

Reuben's son, James Overton Holly, was trained as a shoemaker because the increased competition of hired slaves and the flow of European immigrant "contract labor" into construction work forced the free black into other service-oriented occupations. Shoemaking, when practiced, would help support the next three generations of Holly men. The shoes President Madison wore to his first inauguration in 1809 were products of James Overton Holly's craftsmanship.[4]

A tourist visiting the federal city in the 1820s categorized the capital's occupants as follows: a small group of the "better sort," those who kept boarding houses and their "mutual friends," the subordinate officers of the government, the laboring classes, and free Negroes. Yet in the early years of the District free blacks still enjoyed many of the simple pleasures that would presently be denied their class. They could fish and bathe in the Potomac, admire the caged grizzly bears kept on the White House lawn, listen to the Marine Band concerts, gawk at the visiting groups of Indians, attend the autumn horse races, and stroll along the wide corridors of the new Capitol building. Of course, politically, the free Negro made little headway. District laws inherited from neighboring states prohibited him from voting, holding office, testifying in court against whites, serving on juries, or bearing firearms. And by 1829, the year James Theodore Holly was born to James Overton and Jane Holly, tighter racial restrictions had been imposed by the municipality on the 3,000-member free black population. The Holly family, living in the western part of the federal city near Georgetown, not only faced the usual disenfranchisement and exclusion from the "better jobs," but also had to present papers of freedom and post a "peace" bond of $100 endorsed by two white residents. Other laws were initiated to inhibit further the free black's economic endeavors. An ordinance passed in 1831 ruled that he could receive no license but that of cart, wagon, or hackney driver. Five years later he temporarily was prohibited from operating any new tavern or restaurant.[5]

James Theodore Holly spent the first fifteen years of his life in the District. When he was not yet two, the bloody Nat Turner slave insurrection in Virginia shattered any calm that had prevailed and sharpened racial tensions between the white and black communities in Washington. In September 1835, a full-fledged race riot rocked the city. White rioters, primarily mechanics from the Navy Yard, wrecked the restaurant of Benjamin Snow and then ransacked the homes of free blacks, ostensibly in search of antislavery literature, but "impelled undoubtedly by hostility to the Negro race and the motives of plunder." Nearly all the Negro school houses were partially demolished and some private homes burned.[6]

Public sentiment in the District had been tolerant in allowing free blacks to acquire a partial education. Yet James Overton Holly, a man of more than ordinary intelligence, had never been able to obtain much formal schooling because no opportunities for either public or private training existed in the federal city before 1814. Realizing the importance of education, especially to those of a so-called degraded race, James Overton encouraged his sons to pursue academic as well as shoemaking knowledge. In 1837, at a time when the more timid Washington Negroes still did not dare to send their children to school because of the smoldering racial violence in the community, James Theodore Holly and his brother Joseph enrolled in Dr. John H. Fleet's school. Fleet, a well-educated mulatto, had studied medicine with partial support from the American Colonization Society, a group which hoped to send him to Liberia. After rejecting the idea of emigration, Fleet opened a school in the District. James and Joseph therefore studied under a refined and polished gentleman, a man conceded to be the foremost Negro in culture, intellectual force, and general influence in Washington.[7]

The Hollys lived more than a mile away from the Fleet school, and the brothers, while walking to and from school, were subjected to the flying rocks as well as the taunts of white children and adults. Indeed, throughout the three decades before the Civil War, pupils in all-Negro schools confronted similar situations. But one suspects the rewards for James and Joseph were worth the hostilities incurred. Theirs was a privileged position. At no time prior to the passage of a bill in 1862 to enact public education for District Negroes did more than one black child in ten attend any type of school.[8]

Despite ever-present prejudice, harassment, and violence in the District, James and Joseph flourished. The happiest moments for the Holly brothers were the hours spent with their father gathering nuts and berries in the marshes and thick woods around Washington. Their mother's influence was felt in the sphere of religion. With her, the two boys and their sister Cecilia attended Holy Trinity Catholic Church in Georgetown. No other religious denomination from the earliest history of the District had exhibited such a true, Christian spirit toward the Negro people as did the Roman Catholic church. The pastors of Holy Trinity befriended the poor blacks and recognized no distinctions on account of skin color. The Catholic church freely offered all its privileges to the Negro worshipper, and in the Catholic church's sanctuary the "black" gallery or "nigger pews" found in white Protestant churches did not exist. During the 1830s, the years of the mob, the Catholic churches stood firm and allowed no molestation of their black parishioners.[9]

## II

In 1844 James Overton Holly, at the advanced age of fifty-eight, traveled by ship with his wife and three surviving children to Brooklyn "to be relieved of *some* of the disabilities free colored men labor under in the South." No doubt the senior Holly had wearied of the long residence in an area where every imaginable form of humiliating restriction hampered his personal freedom. Although there had no repetition of the riots of 1835, the tense and restricting climate in the District of Columbia stifled emancipated blacks. James Overton owned no taxable property to tie him to the area. And if he was not aware of the proportional decline of free-black residents in the federal city, he had noted that many whites had urged the corporate authorities to tighten up the city's racial codes to help further curb the growth of this "insolent" class of Negroes. Still another reason behind the Holly family's move was the blossoming racial pride of nineteen-year-old Joseph and his fifteen-year-old brother, James. Both youths longed to take a first step away from their birthplace, a city whose motto seemed to be "no white man can do a wrong to a colored man and no colored man willingly does right to anybody."[10]

James Overton Holly most likely chose Brooklyn because relatives and friends were present in the Negro community there. And Brooklyn presented better business opportunities than Washington for a black craftsman to capitalize on his skills. Because bootmaking was a trade in which it was possible to attract a white clientele, the Hollys rejected the choice of one of the scattered black settlements ringing Brooklyn to establish themselves in the Negro section closest to the waterfront. Once settled, both boys worked at shoemaking alongside their father in his rented shop until the following year, when Joseph opened his own business. The ever-rising rents for commercial space on Brooklyn's busy streets forced many mechanics among the black population of 2,000 to give up their business locations. The repair shops of both Janes Overton and Joseph Holly moved yearly between 1845 and 1849. Those few Negroes with working capital, such as the pharmacist and physician James McCune Smith in Manhattan, bought instead of rented and then lived to see the value of their investments soar.[11]

During the Hollys' years in the Brooklyn–New York City area, the black population slowly declined. Relatively few Negroes migrated into the region because of the open hostility shown them, both by older residents and by the recently arrived immigrants—especially the Irish. Housing for the black population of 13,000 in Manhattan was poor and little better across the East River in Brooklyn. But in Brooklyn, segregation was not as rigid and employment opportunities were enhanced. In fact, blacks living in lower Manhattan often sought jobs in Brooklyn.[12]

Joseph gradually drifted into active involvement in the antislavery movement in New York City and Brooklyn, while James, already dreaming of emigrating from the United States, continued his independent study in the evenings. As early as 1843 James had started spending any extra money he might have on books. At fourteen he was piously preaching to his friends that their money should be used for educational purposes and "not spent for rum, tobacco, and other foolish and hurtful practices." The younger Holly's progress as a scholar attracted the attention of an outspoken and controversial Spanish Roman Catholic priest, the Reverend Felix Varela, of Transfiguration Church in New York City. In the evenings Holly would travel three miles to pursue mathematical and classical lessons under Varela's tutelage, although James did not know "exactly what use I could put those studies to." After finishing his apprenticeship with his father in 1846 and then practicing the shoemaking trade for a year, James sought to put his "night studies" to work. In 1848 he met and so impressed Lewis Tappan, a wealthy businessman, evangelical, and abolitionist, that "Tappen secured for Holley an appointment to clerk for both his own commercial agency and favorite enterprise, the American Missionary Association." Working with the agency Holly received scant wages but accumulated what he later described as "practical contact with the atmosphere of business." The Association also afforded him the chance to meet influential missionary and abolitionist leaders.[13]

Joseph Holly, who in 1947 had been one of Brooklyn's first subscribers to Frederick Douglass's widely read *North Star,* soon became a friend of its black editor and a semiregular correspondent of the paper. Between February and June 1848, Joseph published in the *North Star* a series of five articles entitled "American Slavery." He argued that it was the slave's duty to rebel against his oppressors. Joseph chided the inactivity of his fellow free Negroes, many of whom were former slaves, by asking, in verse, "Is true freedom but to break fetters for your own dear sake?"[14]

Sometime during the latter half of the 1840s James Overton Holly died of consumption, and in the spring of 1850 his widow and the three grown children packed up and moved 400 miles farther north to Burlington, Vermont. It is likely that the change was in response to the Fugitive Slave Act of 1850, against the operation of which free blacks had no legal protection. No doubt the staunch antislavery posture of Vermont was attractive to the family. The congestion of Brooklyn and New York City with accompanying poor sanitation had also been detrimental to James's health and had weakened the constitution of his sister, Cecilia. Thus Vermont, a state of mountains, valleys, streams, and more cows than people, was doubly attractive to the Hollys.[15]

According to Joseph Holly, Burlington was a "beautiful village with clean, lively, orderly inhabitants." Sitting picturesquely on the shores of Lake Champlain with the Ausable river and the Adirondack mountains in the background, their new home offered the Hollys a startling change in racial attitudes. The state had long been tolerant of its small black population. Its constitution made no distinction with regard to color, and Negroes had graduated from Vermont universities—no small feat for that day.[16]

The Hollys, probably the only Negro family in their immediate area, settled comfortably into a rented house in a neighborhood inhabited by French Canadians and Irish of the lower working class. While their mother and sister commenced housekeeping, the two brothers, with aid from Lewis Tappan, began their partnership as "fashionable bootmakers" in the commercial district of the village.[17]

Affairs of a local nature occupied the attention of Burlington's residents. Subjects of debate included the poor road conditions, the grazing of animals in the street, the preservation of shade trees, and the inconveniences caused by barking dogs. Burlington's placid atmosphere, after the negrophobia of Washington and the bustle of Brooklyn, must have been a delightful change for the boys' mother and sister. But the race-proud James and Joseph, while viewing the move to Vermont as prudent, must have missed the black social and cultural institutions found in New York City.[18]

Occupied in earning a living during the daylight hours, the two brothers devoted their evenings to the controversy over the long-dormant black emigration movement, and in particular to the revival of interest in the American Colonization Society under the political leadership of Henry Clay. The American Colonization Society, founded in 1817, had experienced only sputtering success in its campaign to send American Negroes to Liberia. Ideally, the Society's white founders had believed that the free Negro could be transported to the land of his ancestors, thereby ending the dangers from the alarming increase in the free-black population. Slaveholders could then safely and gradually emancipate their chattels and the Negro problem would be solved. Most free blacks, however, were not prepared to endorse a movement with such hypocritical overtones. They believed that the white supporters of colonization only claimed to be motivated by a humanitarian spirit, because these same whites refused to oppose the racial laws existing in both the North and South. In fact, many members of the American Colonization Society supported racial barriers in the United States to make the prospect of being transported abroad more inviting to the free blacks. It is true that some whites hoped that the establishment of an African homeland would ultimately encourage slaveholders to free their bondsmen. Others in the Society looked upon the removal of free blacks as an easy way to strengthen the institution of slavery. To most free Negroes the Society was too eclectic in both its membership and its ideology to be inviting. On the one hand Negroes were told that theirs was a depraved race, a "living pestilence" whose elevation in America was impossible; yet at the same time they were encouraged to believe that the Negro had sufficient mental ability to colonize and Christianize in Africa.[19]

As early as February 1850 Joseph Holly had addressed, through the columns of the *North Star,* a sarcastic "open letter" to Henry Clay and the members of the American Colonization Society. In this letter he begged Clay to pardon the criticism from one whom the Society proposed "to benefit." He asked what crime

American blacks had committed to cause their removal: "Is it only the color of their skin?" Despite prejudice, Joseph argued, Negroes still had a greater opportunity for advancement in this country than in underdeveloped Liberia. He stated, or perhaps threatened, that "we intend to go where you go, die where you die, and be buried in your place of burial."[20]

James Theodore Holly's own feelings about the Society and Liberian colonization were directly opposed to his brother's. Recalling that his former teacher, Dr. Fleet, had been educated by the Society, and reacting to the invitation printed in its paper, *The African Repository*, for "colored men" to express their opinions on colonization, James wrote a long letter in June 1850 to William McClain, secretary of the Society. He rejected outright the criticism of Joseph and his friends, confessed to McClain his pride in Liberian independence, and asserted his faith in the future greatness of that country. "I have concluded that I would not hesitate to emigrate to Liberia, provided I could make myself useful to the community." Holly asked McClain for financial support to allow him, preparatory to leaving for Africa, to study medicine, especially hydropathy and homeopathy. Secretary McClain responded to James's inquiry, pleaded a lack of immediate funds for medical students, and encouraged his correspondent to continue his education and then go to Liberia either as a teacher or as a professor at the Society's new college. But McClain was so intrigued by the "very intelligent correspondent in Burlington" who could write "a really *first-class* letter" that he wrote to Joseph Tracy of the Society's Massachusetts branch to tell him about Holly, "a man worth looking after and *perhaps* doing something for."[21]

The two Hollys now began to debate before Burlington audiences the question, "Can the colored people of the United States best elevate their condition by remaining in this country or by emigrating to Liberia?" Joseph maintained that "we are here and here we mean to remain; we can't be coaxed, cheated, hissed, or kicked out of this country; we look with unmitigated disapprobation upon such propositions . . . as the American Colonization Society." In more moderate but no less earnest tones, James' Theodore Holly, with the ongoing fugitive slave debate in the nation's capital in mind, insisted that only by emigrating could the American Negro be really free. The test of time would place the much criticized Society "in a different and higher view by all who take an interest in our race, especially we the free colored people of the United States." Twenty-one years of age, the inexperienced Holly had not yet accepted the almost universal feeling of Northern free blacks that the Society was not a workable emigration vehicle.[22]

Sincere though he was in his hopes for Liberia, young James Holly also wanted a Society-supported education for himself. No doubt he was restless; "beautiful Burlington," even with its enlightened racial climate, was meant to be no more than a temporary stop in his travels. Also, his pro-Society stance had won few, if any, converts among Vermont's small black population. While proud of his craftsmanship in shoemaking, Holly had no desire to spend his life making shoes, "proscribed from all honorable employment by the white race." He yearned to use not his hands but his mind to elevate himself and his race.[23]

# Search for a Place: Canada

In 1850 a wave of apprehension passed through the free Negro community of the United States. A momentary truce in Congress between Northern and Southern politicians had allowed the passage of a new fugitive slave bill which imperiled the safety of free blacks nationwide. The Fugitive Slave Act of 1850 barred Negro testimony in court and made the aiding of a runaway slave a federal offense. It was now quite possible for a free-born Negro to be "mistakenly" identified as a fugitive and carried South.[1]

## I

Reacting to the Fugitive Slave Act of 1850, many de facto free blacks, those who had escaped from bondage, looked to Canada as a haven from the hired slave catchers thought to be prowling the Northern states. One such person who crossed into Canada for relief was Henry Bibb. Bibb, thirty-five years old, was without formal education, but was nonetheless an engaging, forceful, and untiring worker in the antislavery movement. Born in slavery, he had been an incorrigible runaway and had consequently been sold six separate times. After his final escape in 1840 he made his way to Detroit, where he joined the Liberty Party and lectured for antislavery forces. With the passage of the new fugitive slave bill, Bibb moved across the river to the Sandwich–Windsor area of Canada West. Here he worked to attract black emigrants.[2]

On January 1, 1851, Bibb began publication from Sandwich of the *Voice of the Fugitive,* a semimonthly newspaper dedicated to the "immediate and unconditional abolition of chattel slavery everywhere." He also meant to persuade "every oppressed person of color in the United States to settle in Canada where the laws make no distinction among men based on complexion." In subsequent issues Bibb trumpeted the virtues of Canada: "her unlimited tracts of timber, her mild and congenial climate . . . her beautiful lakes, rivers, fruit, fish, and game." The *Voice of the Fugitive* also pointed out the success of blacks who had already crossed into Canada, portraying them as "owners and tillers" of the soil, taxpayers, and advocates of schools, churches, and temperance societies. In Burlington, Vermont, the early issues of Bibb's paper came into the hands of James Theodore Holly, a voracious reader and a young man in search of a place to display his growing zeal for a black nationality. His brief flirtation with the white-controlled Liberian colonization scheme had passed and had now been supplanted by an interest in voluntary emigration to Canada.[3]

A letter published in the *Voice of the Fugitive* on May 7, 1851, represented Holly's first venture into print. Dubbing himself a "voluntary correspondent," Holly—as yet unknown to the leadership of the free-black community—condemned the Fugitive Slave Act and predicted a dissolution of the American Union and the emancipation of the bondsmen. Looking for a positive aspect to the new law, he saw it as a stimulus to American blacks to move to the freedom of Canada. "There is no time more expedient, no place more proper, and no persons more suitable than the Canadian refugees to organize and facilitate in the escape and settlement of other blacks to Canada."[4]

Henry Bibb had been at work on a plan to attract refugees to Canada. In November 1850, encouraged by the increase in Negro movement across the border, Bibb and other blacks of the Windsor–Sandwich area organized a "Fugitive Union," whose aim was to enable every escapee from slavery to become a landowner. The Union would buy up 30,000 acres of land and then resell it to the fugitives in lots not to exceed twenty-five acres. One-third of the income derived from the sales would be channeled into the education of the settlers and their children, the other two-thirds into investment in more land.[5]

Holly, in Burlington, took note of the project and declared it the duty of all American blacks to support the Union and to regard Bibb as the head of all future efforts. He called for his people to leave the "drudging employment of menials" and locate in the primitive communities of Canada. To Holly, the prospect of Canadian emigration now held out more hope to free blacks than did far-off Liberia. Canada was on the North American continent in close proximity to the slave states. The climate was similar to that of the United States and, most importantly, it was an alternative that blacks could adopt and pursue on their own terms. Finally, as he wrote to the *Voice*, a vigorous pursuit of Canadian colonization would "hang like a black cloud" over the United States.[6]

Disagreement was no stranger to the free black community of North America, and the one issue certain to cause division was colonization. The *Voice of the Fugitive* was in direct editorial opposition to *Frederick Douglass' Paper*, the leading Negro organ in the United States. Carefully avoiding any references to Bibb's paper, Douglass described the emigration of free blacks to Canada and urged that "now was [*sic*] a time when every intelligent colored American was needed at home . . . to stand between our people and the hateful scheme of colonization."[7]

Ignoring his black opponents, Bibb continued to steer a course towards emigration, and Holly followed in his wake. In July 1851 the *Voice of the Fugitive* issued a call for a North American Convention of Negroes to meet in Toronto the following September. Bibb printed the topics for discussion, labeling them "ideas from our correspondents." One item in particular, "to recommend the emigration of free people of color from the United States to Canada," greatly interested the *Voice*'s correspondent in Burlington. In Vermont, however, Holly was in the minority of a minority in his desire for emigration. Either interest was so slight among the Vermont Negroes, or the opposition so active under his brother Joseph, that James was able to secure only one other signature, in addition to that of his aged mother, for the state's "call" to the North American Convention—and a lack of money kept him at home.[8]

The convention met September 11–13, with fifty-one delegates attending from five states and Canada. Bibb as president effectively controlled and directed the proceedings. Among the members was the sharp-tongued, race-conscious Martin R. Delany of Pittsburgh. Opposing Bibb, Delany worked to defeat a resolution encouraging Canadian colonization, calling migration impolitic and contrary to the wishes of most American blacks.[9]

On its last day the convention unanimously adopted Holly's plan to form a "great league of colored people" of North and South America and the West Indies. This league would advocate the abolition of slavery and the protection of the common rights of Negroes throughout the world. Holly's proposals, read in his absence by J. G. Fisher of Toronto, envisioned a North American and West Indian Federal Agricultural Union with a provision for the cooperative purchase and distribution of land in these areas. Holly believed that the free-black population of the United States was in danger of being blotted out of existence, "taxed without representation, practically denied the electoral franchise, denied the right in many states of protecting their chastity, liberty, lives, or property." He would give his people a remedy. Let them emigrate to Canada or the British West Indies and then bring their products—grain, cotton, and sugar—in direct competition with the agricultural goods of the slaveholding South and the racially intolerant North. This proposal marked an unmistakable break with previous antislavery programs. Holly's league would legislate for the interests of all "colored peoples in the United States and the Canadian provinces" and "adopt measures for their advancement *irrespective of any other association.*" Blacks should direct their own antislavery movement because "all other persons who may be friendly to our race, should remember a people understands their [*sic*] own wants best themselves."[10]

The convention appointed a committee of seven, headed by Bibb, to lay the groundwork for future meetings. Because four of the seven members had not been present in Toronto, the bulk of the postconvention work fell on Bibb's shoulders. And

Bibb proceeded, whether by accident or design, to bring Holly into the organization. He had become increasingly impressed by the diligence and zeal of his Burlington correspondent and also, no doubt, by Holly's expressed loyalty to Bibb's ideas. The editor turned to Holly to help with a preamble and constitution for the North American League. Thus at age twenty-two Holly began his move into prominence in the free-black community of North America. A preview of the finished constitution appeared in the *Voice of the Fugitive* on February 26, 1852, along with the editor's promise that the next issue of the paper would offer "J. T. Holly's approval and explanation upon the whole document."[11]

What the next issue did carry was Bibb's announcement that Holly would henceforth act as the paper's corresponding editor and traveling agent. Holly had been at a dead end in Vermont and was anxious to join in a work that promised relief to "the whole destiny of the Africo–American race." Bibb commissioned him to travel and lecture in the East to stir up interest in emigration to Canada and to enlist new subscribers for the *Voice of the Fugitive*. Holly and his young wife, the former Charlotte Ann Gordon of Burlington, made a six-week lecture tour in five eastern states, then arrived in early June 1852 at the *Voice*'s new home in Windsor, Canada West. Two weeks later Bibb announced Holly's appointment as associate editor and proprietor, and Holly's name appeared on the paper's masthead.[12]

## II

Windsor in 1852 was a Canadian village in the process of becoming a small city. Three-quarters of a mile across the river from Detroit, Windsor's hastily erected shops swarmed with tradesmen from the United States, French Canadian farmers, and refugees from slavery. Noise from the construction of new buildings and from the expanded trade along the waterfront filled the air, and the townspeople eagerly awaited completion of the tracks of the Great Western Railway. On the surface, at least, the Windsor region seemed a place where the black man could seek both economic success and social freedom.[13]

Literally before he could unpack his bags Holly found himself in sole charge of the *Voice*. He was also expected to run a printing business that supplemented the small income derived from newspaper subscriptions. There is no indication that he faltered. With the senior editor absent on the lecture circuit, Holly immersed himself in the activities of the black communities of Windsor and Detroit.

The second issue of the *Voice of the Fugitive* under Holly's direction carried the announcement that the final constitution of the North American League, now to be called the "American Continental and West Indies League," had been drawn up. The first "auxiliary" would be formed in Windsor. Interested parties were urged to apply to the corresponding secretary, Holly himself, for more details. A journal of the proceedings in 1851, together with the constitution, was in preparation for the press and would be published "as soon as the prospects of the League are sufficiently encouraging." Evidently the League was stillborn, for it was never mentioned again.[14]

Holly's association with Henry Bibb involved him in another "Bibb enterprise," the Refugee Home Society. The controversy over this organization would last for more than a decade, long after Bibb was dead and Holly safely in Haiti. It divided the black population along the Windsor–Detroit frontier, and helped destroy the *Voice of the Fugitive.*

Before examining Holly's role in this we need to sketch the Society's history. By the mid-1840s a number of Negroes already lived along the Canadian–United States border, where they struggled to find employment or squatted on the land. Most were ignorant, penniless refugees from slavery. As their number increased, white philanthropists and abolitionists in the Detroit area worked to ease their economic plight by collecting food and clothing and, more important, by establishing a permanent settlement for the fugitives. An outgrowth of these endeavors was the Fugitive Union, which in 1851 merged with and took the name of the predominantly white-controlled Refugee Home Society.[15]

When Holly settled in Windsor the Society, in which Henry Bibb and his wife Mary represented the Negroes, was still in the process of perfecting its organization. It had, nevertheless, already launched ambitious plans to buy 50,000 acres of Canadian farm land to be doled out to refugee families in tracts of twenty-five acres. As many as 2,000 acres were presently purchased, with half of it immediately resold to 150 families. But the Refugee Home Society, with its program for the rehabilitation and training of the fugitive, split the Windsor black community. A faction favoring the Society was led by Bibb and Holly, with their paper as its organ. The opposition, headed by Miss Mary A. Shadd, militant and indefatigable, fought the program at every opportunity. Young Holly threw himself into the thick of the Society fracas. With Bibb frequently absent, he wrote much of the *Voice*'s editorial support for the Society.[16]

It is difficult to analyze the mass of conflicting, fragmented, and questionable arguments offered for and against the Refugee Home Society. The best case against the Society was that there was no need for such an organization. The Society's land was more expensive than that available independently, and its terms violated the Negro's rights in that it could repossess assigned land. Mary A. Shadd considered the fund-raising agents of the Society no better than extortionists, and Bibb and Holly tools of Detroit whites.[17]

Holly attributed the antagonism in the black community either to the free-born Negroes or the refugees who had acquired Canadian property for themselves, because neither group could participate in the Refugee Home Society. Those being criticized should not be aggrieved, he said, for to attempt to help all people at once was utopian fantasy. "Reform," he observed, "when presented in its simplest and most feasible shape, may be realized on a partial scale in the present. With this reformers must be content, accepting it as a pledge and basis for the future." To those blacks who objected to the segregated communities established by the Society, Holly argued that segregation was desirable. Though he wanted social distinctions based on color to be eradicated, he was skeptical that this would or could ever happen. Now was not the time. If barriers were to be torn down, the first move would have to be made by the Negro himself, "in a state of freedom, after he becomes *thoroughly educated,* and the *personal* state of slavery shall be lost." Holly was convinced that the Society was beneficial to blacks. And because he believed he was right he did not shrink from an increasingly unpopular cause.[18]

To counteract the *Voice's* support for the Society, Mary A. Shadd and Samuel Ringgold Ward raised enough money to print one issue of a newspaper, the *Provincial Freeman.* It appeared on March 24, 1853, promising to become a weekly if it obtained a "sufficient number" of cash subscribers. The entire issue was devoted to criticism of the Society, which it claimed misrepresented the condition of refugees in Canada. Preaching self-help views, the newspaper declared that jobs were available to fugitives. But the controversy had become so bitter that it led to violence and death. At a meeting of Holly's debating club in early March 1853, a young black was killed in a fight. The *Voice* denounced the act as "A Deed of Blood," charging those Negroes interested in destroying the *Voice* and replacing it with the *Provincial Freeman* with inciting disruption in Windsor. The *Freeman* ignored the murder and hinted that the mere presence of Bibb and Holly caused more division among the Negro population than any physical assaults by other individuals.[19]

South of the border, *Frederick Douglass' Paper* had already expressed its amazement that Bibb and Ward, "two champions of freedom and progress of the colored people of Canada," could be at open war with each other. Douglass suggested that the whole controversy, if ignored, would adjust itself. Sensibly, he advised fugitives to secure land where they received the most favorable terms.[20]

Unfortunately, events were not resolved this easily in Windsor. The single issue of the *Provincial Freeman* in 1853 portended bad times for the *Voice of the Fugitive* and her editors. Much of the black community in Windsor had always been indifferent to any newspaper, even one published by and for Negroes. Now many of the *Voice's* original subscribers were put off by the paper's persistent advocacy of the Refugee Home Society and were increasingly interested in a new and more independent black newspaper such as the *Provincial Freeman.*[21]

## III

Despite the difficulties over the Refugee Home Society, Holly obviously enjoyed his new job in journalism and the prestige that went with it. He had given himself to this vocation with unbounded enthusiasm. Proud of his literary achievements, he sent copies of the *Voice* to his brother Joseph, who now lived in Rochester, New York, at the right hand of Frederick Douglass. Joseph, able to compose poetry and to lecture against slavery, prided himself that he had not deserted the shoemaker's bench, an occupation he felt was a more "democratic" employment than that of editor. Joseph playfully mocked his younger brother's "starched stiff neck dignity, his measured oracular words measured out like precious ointment."[22]

Editor Holly praised Windsor as "beautiful, high and healthy ... an important place for trade and traffic," though he could not help but compare its "underdeveloped" state with the "industrious neighbors on the other side of the border." Holly found time aside from his editorial and printing chores to form a town debating society, to attend Bibb's antislavery group, and to take over the leadership of a Masonic lodge in Detroit. When the time came to celebrate West Indies Emancipation Day on August 1, 1853, Holly and Bibb controlled the program committee and used the occasion to defend the Refugee Home Society.[23]

Holly, contrary to his expectations, did not find Canada free from negrophobia. It was true that the "full odor of the filthy stench of prejudice" found in the United States was not present in Canada, and that discrimination was legally forbidden. Yet in reality the distinction between life in Canada and life in the United States could be less than precise for the Negro. Holly was ready to attack editorially any white man or organization that discriminated against blacks. The *Voice* carried on a continuous battle with the scurrilous Amherstburg *Courier,* a paper dedicated to keeping Canada for the Canadians. But neither the *Voice* nor any individual could effectively stifle the antagonism directed toward the black emigrant. With the increased emigration of the 1850s the racial sentiments of whites in Canada West too often mirrored those of their nearby neighbors in the United States. Some native Canadians believed the black to be too transient to help the frontier communities, while other whites decried the permanence of the newcomers. Yet throughout Holly's stay in Canada West the blacks were not segregated. They lived interspersed with whites and were grudgingly accepted by most whites except the Irish.[24]

In 1853 the editors of the *Voice of the Fugitive* started a third year of uninterrupted publication, an almost unprecedented achievement for a North American Negro newspaper. They hoped not only to continue publication, but also to expand from bimonthly to a weekly paper by increasing the number of readers and the price of subscriptions. But the *Voice* remained a bimonthly. Although it billed itself as the "faithful exponent and monitor of interest of the colored people," the paper continued to alienate a portion of the Negro community in Windsor.[25]

While the Refugee Home Society controversy remained very much alive, a new issue arose to divide further the supporters of Bibb and Holly from those of Mary A. Shadd and Samuel Ward. Ward called for a convention to meet in London, Canada West, in April 1853 to promote "elevation and progress among the colored inhabitants of Canada." Bibb and Holly opposed this convention as being not nationalistic enough for their purposes. They claimed it would be nothing more than a vehicle for encouraging the renewed operation of the *Provincial Freeman*. The activities of the London Convention were played down in the *Voice*, and Holly and Bibb countered with a call for a meeting in June 1853 at Amherstburg, Canada West. Ostensibly, the Amherstburg Convention was called to seek the "general improvement" of Canadian Negroes. But the issues actually discussed were emigration to Canada and the health and future of the *Voice of the Fugitive*, which the London meeting had found "not respectable and not representative of the colored Canadians."[26]

The proceedings at the sparsely attended Amherstburg Convention reflected the growing disillusionment and changing interests of some Canadian Negroes, particularly Holly. Stung by white prejudice in Canada and by the criticism of Mary A. Shadd, Holly was now searching for a place where American and Canadian Negroes could create a separate national identity and a power base of their own. The report of the committee on emigration, of which Holly was chairman, announced that a revolution by blacks in the United States "is the boldest and probably the most glorious alternative for colored Americans to follow." The committee then turned to emigration as a sound substitute for revolution. After paying lip service to emigration to Canada, Holly advanced the option of emigration to the West Indies in general and Haiti in particular.[27]

In two years James Theodore Holly had emerged from the shadow of his older brother Joseph and become, at the age of twenty-three, a spokesman for at least a segment of the free-black community. Although he had been involved in two apparent failures, the North American League and the Refugee Home Society, he had gained experience that would prove useful in the future.

During his apprenticeship under Henry Bibb, Holly had come to believe that the black man could not achieve "person freedom" until all sense of his subservience and inferiority to the white man had vanished. To achieve this goal, Holly now maintained that the Negro must separate himself completely from his white antagonists. And in Holly's view, Haiti was the logical place to accomplish this segregation.

# III

# Change in Direction

Holly became increasingly involved in the organized meetings of the black emigration movement. Many of the grandiose plans proposed in conventions, many by Holly himself, never materialized. Yet unlike many of his contemporaries he did not merely attend the sessions, participate in debate, vote on specific measures, and then return home to await the next coming together. Instead Holly resolved to separate himself permanently from his homeland by emigrating to Haiti.

## I

A convention of free Negroes gathered as early as 1830 in Philadelphia "to devise ways and means" of bettering the living conditions of their people. Similar groups of Negroes, often joined by white abolitionists, continued to meet on local or state levels during the next twenty-three years. In an effort to coordinate the state conventions, Negroes representing various states assembled in Rochester, New York, in 1853 to lay detailed plans for the advancement of the free blacks of America. Included in the delegation were a few advocates of emigration, such as William C. Munroe and James Whitfield. But they were greatly outnumbered by delegates, including James Holly's brother, Joseph, who agreed with Frederick Douglass that Negroes could best combat racism in the United States by remaining in the United States. The Rochester convention voted to form a Negro national college, library, and consumer union, but realization of these hopes was doomed by the chronic dearth of funds, the apathy among the Negro masses, and the rising interest in emigration.[1]

The sessions at Rochester had scarcely closed before emigrationist sentiment prompted a proposal for another national convention, this one to be held in Cleveland in August 1854. The "Call," which was endorsed by a band of free blacks more militant than Douglass, specifically limited attendance to those who favored emigration in the Western Hemisphere. This restriction set off a heated debate among Northern Negroes. The most eloquent criticism, by Douglass and his assistant, William J. Watkins, appeared in *Frederick Douglass' Paper*. Arguments in favor of the meeting, written mainly by James Whitfield, were published in the *Voice of the Fugitive.* The pieces on both sides were drawn together by a Detroit Negro, M. T. Newsome, and republished in January 1854 in a pamphlet entitled *Arguments Pro and Con on the Call for a National Emigration Convention.* James Theodore Holly wrote the introduction to the pamphlet. In it Holly paid lip service to the Rochester meeting, one of the "grandest arrays of talent and wisdom ever assembled on this continent." He also credited Douglass with establishing a national organization for a "denationalized people." But he left little doubt where his own allegiance lay. According to Holly, the rising interest of blacks in emigration made the goals of the Rochester meeting obsolete.

Appended to the Newsome pamphlet was an annotated list of possible locations for colonization by American Negroes. Among the descriptions were Henry Bibb's of Jamaica, "his next choice after Canada," and Holly's of Haiti, "the first nationality established by our race." Holly wrote that "every colored man should feel bound to sustain the national existence of Hayti." He also argued, as he would often in the next seven years, that emigration to the Black Republic by large numbers of American Negroes would both strengthen the government of Haiti and give hope and pride to those Negroes remaining in the United States.[2]

Holly's involvement in planning and promoting the Cleveland convention was pushed aside temporarily by the more mundane task of feeding himself, his wife, and their young child. The *Voice of the Fugitive,* after three years of continuous publication, had been discontinued at the end of 1853. Rising expenses and a drop in circulation, attributed in part to the paper's stubborn endorsement of the Refugee Home Society, had hastened its demise. The coeditor, Henry Bibb, wanted to travel the lecture circuit on a full-time basis, and Holly himself had grown restless in Canada. The association with Bibb and the *Voice* had, however, been helpful to young Holly, giving him a chance to speak before large audiences, to discipline his rambling writing style, to learn the printing trade, and, most of all, to win a growing reputation among the free blacks of Canada and Northern United States.[3]

Holly moved back to the United States. The Negroes of Buffalo, New York, had requested that a black man be appointed principal of the only Negro school in the city, and Holly took the job. His tenure was short. He may have offended parents with his frequent lectures in support of emigration. What is certain is that he absented himself often from school, as did many of his 216 pupils, and incurred the displeasure of the superintendent of the Buffalo schools, whose annual report for 1854 described Holly's school as "not in as good a condition as under its former principal, either through want of proper discipline or on account of dissension among its patrons."[4]

Late in July 1854 Holly returned to visit Henry Bibb, who had been ill since March. He attended the celebration of West Indies emancipation held annually in Windsor

on August 1. The announcement of Bibb's death on the morning of the first cur-
tailed the festivities planned for the day. A meeting was called and Holly was asked
to eulogize Bibb. Part of this panegyric was later printed in *Frederick Douglass'
Paper,* the first and last time any item over Holly's signature appeared in that
journal. After helping Bibb's widow, Mary—herself an activist in the emigration
movement—settle her late husband's private affairs, Mrs. Bibb, Holly, and a large
Detroit delegation including Holly's close friends, Munroe and William Lambert,
journeyed to the Cleveland Emigration Convention.[5]

One hundred and two delegates from twelve states and Canada answered the
thirteen-month-old "Call to Convention" at Cleveland. But the idea of a national
meeting to promote emigration had been so thoroughly criticized in Negro communities in the preceding months that several of the original signers of the "Call"
failed to appear. Delegates were mostly from midwestern states, with Holly the
only one from New York. The most established and prosperous Negroes of the
East Coast were antiemigrationist and endorsed the "stay-at-home" policy of the
Rochester meeting. In fact, *Frederick Douglass' Paper* condemned the Cleveland
delegates as "unwise" and "unintelligent." Responding in kind, they pronounced
Douglass "illiberal and supercilious" for his criticism.[6]

After forbidding any remarks from the floor that did not deal with emigration,
the convention in three days of proceedings adopted a platform, considered the
establishment of a national literary quarterly, and set up a national board of commissioners to direct emigration. A speech by Martin R. Delany on the "Political
Destiny of the Colored Race in the American Continent" highlighted the meeting.
Formerly the editor of his own newspaper as well as coeditor with Frederick
Douglass, Delany had been active in opposing colonization as late as 1851. Now
he represented a forceful voice for emigration. Delany's speech emphasized thay
"the liberty of no man is secure, who does not control his own political destiny,"
and called for American Negroes to remedy their insecurity by settling in the
West Indies or Central or South America. With help from black American emigrants as leaders, he said, the "colored races," both Indian and African, could gain
control of those territories.[7]

Holly was continuously active in Cleveland. He served on both the committee on
credentials—the body responsible for admitting only those delegates who promised to favor emigration—and the committee to nominate permanent officers.
The officers turned out to include his friend Munroe as president, Mrs. Bibb as
vice-president, and Holly himself as one of the secretaries. Holly's influence was
also evident in the resolution that "the first Day of January each year be observed
as a day of celebration, being the Anniversary of Haytian independence."

Holly, William Lambert, and James Whitfield (who was not in attendance) had
drawn up and presented to the convention a plan for a quarterly literary journal

tentatively called the *Africo-American Repository*. The *Repository* was to represent and be supported by proponents of emigration. It was also to present the ideas of "the ablest colored writers in both hemisphere," men whose literary achievements would "bring the evidence of progress before those who deny such progress." Despite the expectations of its supporters, plans for the journal were shelved until the next convention in 1856.

The major work was done in "secret" session chaired by Delany. One decision was to establish a permanent national board of commissioners based in Pittsburgh. All the national officers were required to live there, but two commissioners were designated for each state, Holly being elected to represent New York. The other principal decision related to emigration. In a letter written many years later, Holly explained it thus:

> Dr. Delany headed the emigration party that desired to go to the Niger Valley in Africa, Whitfield the party which preferred to go to Central America and Holly the party which preferred to go to Hayti. All these parties were recognized and embraced by the Convention. Dr. Delany was given a commission to go to Africa in the Niger Valley, Whitfield to go to Central America and Holly to Hayti to enter into negotiations with authorities of these various countries for Negro emigrants and to report to future conventions.

Although Holly proved to be the first to carry out his commission, his trip had to await his finding funds to undertake it. They would not come from the national board of commissioners, a body which existed on a financial shoestring throughout its five-year life and could not underwrite travel.[8]

## II

Holly later explained why he had chosen Haiti. As a youth in Washington he had met Roman Catholic missionaries who had returned from Haiti. "The discussions which I heard on the subject were sufficient to feed my ambition. I became absorbed with the hope of going to Hayti as a missionary." He reprinted many favorable reports on Haiti during his tenure as coeditor of the *Voice of the Fugitive*. His devotion was also apparent in his sensitivity to criticism about Haiti. Thus after his brother Joseph mocked the Black Republic and her "weak-noodled" Emperor, Faustin Soulouque I, James replied by dedicating a Masonic lodge in Detroit to the greatness of Haiti and her monarch. In a sense, Joseph's death in Rochester on January 3, 1855, after a six-month struggle with consumption, strengthened James's bent toward Haiti by removing a personal obstacle to his emigration plans. That a person he had loved and respected had been so opposed to emigration must have restrained his activities somewhat. The brothers exemplified the best of the leadership of the two groups of free Negroes in the United

States during the 1850s. They were united in their love for the black race and their wish to see it uplifted. They had differed only over how that advancement could be achieved.[9]

The idea of black solidarity attracted Holly. Haiti was the only independent, Negro-controlled nation in the New World. The very name, the Black Republic, was alluring. Haiti, which blacks had wrestled away from the whites, offered the American Negro a chance to reestablish pride and confidence in his own abilities, a confidence and pride that had been lost during three centuries of bondage to white men. Holly remained firm throughout his lifetime in the belief that the best hope for the American Negro was to separate himself from the white race. And the existence of the Republic of Haiti vindicated this ideal. Holly was aware that the popular image of Haiti was that of a semisavage, caste-ridden, politically unstable, and poverty-stricken country. Yet as a race patriot he chose to look on the positive side of Haitian history.

For Holly the year 1855 was a turning point. In January his immediate family, including now his elderly mother, Jane, moved from Buffalo to Detroit. In Detroit he completed independent ministerial studies and began his career as a clergyman in the Protestant Episcopal church. His new occupation, in conjunction with his devotion to Haiti, set the course for his life. This strong-willed, energetic man was now committed to both the creation of a black nationality and the propagation of the Episcopal faith.

It is important to understand why Holly rejected Catholicism and made his spiritual home in the Episcopal church. From his earliest memory, Holly had believed in God. Shepherded by his mother, he had been baptized in the Roman Catholic church in Washington, took his first communion there, and was confirmed. After his family moved to Brooklyn, he accompanied his mother, sister, and brother to the Church of the Transfiguration in lower Manhattan. The pastor of that church, impressed by the raw intelligence of the black youth, gave James a Bible, his first, and even considered sending him to Rome to prepare for the priesthood. Holly recalled in later life that his study of this gift Bible, full though it was of "explanatory notes in the Roman Catholic sense, gradually weaned me away from the unscriptural ways of that church."[19]

In Burlington, Vermont, on Good Friday 1851, Holly accompanied a white friend to her confirmation at St. Paul's Episcopal Church. This ceremony, performed by Bishop John Henry Hopkins, awakened Holly to the "catholicity" of the Protestant Episcopal church, and the bishop's book entitled *The Primitive Church* convinced him that Episcopalianism was free from "Popish" errors and perversions. After he moved to Canada in 1852, Holly remained interested in this denomination, even though it did not really want black members. Appropriately enough, his first editorial in the *Voice of the Fugitive* offered an "incredulous" comment on the plea of the Episcopal bishop of Pennsylvania, Alonzo Potter, for his state convention to admit Negro delegates.[11]

In Windsor Holly came under the influence of William C. Munroe, pastor of tiny, all-black St. Matthew's Episcopal Church in Detroit. At Munroe's urging Holly renounced Roman Catholicism in 1852 and was confirmed into the Protestant Episcopal church by Bishop Samuel McCroskey of the Diocese of Michigan. Twelve months later McCroskey admitted him as a candidate for Holy Orders. Holly continued his theological education in Buffalo by means of private study with William Shelton, rector of that city's most prominent Episcopal church. He returned to the Detroit area in 1855, ready to be advanced to the diaconate, and the ceremony was performed by McCroskey on the morning of June 17. Holly was the fourteenth member of his race to take ordinational vows in the Protestant Episcopal church.[12]

Three weeks from the day of his ordination as deacon, Holly arrived in New York City to solicit funds from the foreign committee of the Episcopal church for a brief "exploratory" trip to Haiti that might, he hoped, culminate in the appointment of himself and Munroe as missionaries to the Black Republic. His mission was twofold, to examine Haiti as a possible field for Christian labor and, acting under the instructions of the board of commissioners, to "establish communications between the colored people of the United States" and their brethren in the West Indies. Holly did receive private donations from a few Episcopal clergy and laymen, but the national board of commissioners had offered him little more than a paper commission financed by a dream.[13]

After a tedious voyage of three weeks, Holly disembarked in Port-au-Prince, Haiti, on August 3, 1855. Completely ignorant of the French language, he was befriended by John Hepburn, an expatriate merchant from Virginia, and Judge Emil Ballette, an English-educated Haitian. Through their influence official conferences were arranged with the British consul, the emperor's chamberlain, and the secretary of the interior, who in turn presented Holly to the emperor of Haiti, Faustin Soulouque I. Born a slave, Faustin worked his way up through the army, won the presidency as a compromise candidate, and then promptly appointed himself monarch for life. Not a brilliant or charismatic leader, the corpulent emperor managed to use the splendor of his court and the power of his private army to keep the restive population in hand and to impress outside visitors.[14]

Holly found the government of Soulouque mildly interested in a proposal to settle Negroes from the United States in Haiti. Holly asked the Haitian authorities to grant homesteads and equal civil and religious right to American emigrants. He sought to relieve potential settlers from military service for seven years and to allow immigrants to import tools, furniture, and other personal possessions duty free. In return the national board of commissioners promised to send at least two hundred families annually for five years. The secretary of the interior asked that he stay several months so that he might submit his proposition to the legislative assembly, but Holly did not have the money to remain long in Haiti. Before departing he "pledged the honor of the Board [of Commissioners] that myself or another commissioner should return to finish the negotiations I had announced."[15]

From Haiti Holly sent a lengthy descriptive letter to Samuel Denison, the foreign secretary of the board of missions of the Protestant Episcopal church, and on September 10, two days after his return to New York, he submitted a final report. These documents related the "splendid opportunity" for an Episcopal mission to Haiti. Holly elaborated on the weaknesses of the other Protestant churches there, especially the Baptists and the African Methodists. Their "usages do not strike the Haitian mind as being religious worship." The English Wesleyan mission was the most successful because of the "order and decency of the liturgy of the Church of England which is used by the Wesleyans." The Roman Catholic church, nominally controlling the majority of Haitians, was corrupt and out of favor with the emperor. The day after Holly interviewed the Roman Catholic prefect of Port-au-Prince, the latter was "suspended from his duties by order of the Emperor, for being guilty of fornication." Only women attended the Roman worship, Holly reported. The men of Haiti "gratified their religious sentiment" through the symbolism and ceremony of the Masonic lodge. In visiting these temples Holly had been assured that Haitian Masons would flock to Episcopal services. Holly pleaded with Denison and the foreign committee to send himself and one other missionary to Haiti and to provide for the fitting out of "a decent place of worship."[16]

While he awaited the decision of the foreign committee on the question of a permanent mission to Haiti, Holly was unemployed except for occasional day labor on the wharves of New York City. In the evenings he repeatedly delivered a lecture entitled "The Religious Wants of Hayti" and at the close took up a collection to help support his mother, wife, and two young daughters. The speech, which he hoped to present to white as well as black Episcopalians all over the country, acknowledged the existence of "religious superstitions" and called for the church to enter Haiti and for American Negroes "to carry a pure faith and a higher civilization" to the Black Republic.[17]

A trip which Holly took to New Haven, Connecticut, to address the Literary Society of Colored Young Men produced quite a different lecture, one more highly emotional and much more revealing. "A Vindication of the Capacity of the Negro Race for Self Government and Civilized Progress" ignored the subject of religion and concentrated on the goal of black pride. Without discounting the increased humanity shown Negroes by abolitionists and others, Holly saw the greater number of white men still treating the Negro as subhuman. Even many of the "pseudo-humanitarians" possessed "in their heart of hearts a secret infidelity to the real quality of the black man."

One feature of the New Haven lecture was a grand and superficial history of Haiti. Holly skimmed over the problems of despotism, the black–mulatto relationship, and the continuous political upheaval on the island since its independence and presented a half-hearted defense of the monarchy of Faustin Soulouque I. The personal liberty and general welfare of the citizens of Haiti were safer under a monarchy than they would be under a democracy, Holly maintained, because monarchs were held individually responsible for their sins, whereas responsibility in a "bastard democracy" like that of the United States was only collective. "The American People permit a vagabond set of politicians to disgrace the nation and tolerate such odious laws as the Fugitive Slave Bill, violating the Writ of Habeas Corpus and other sacred guarantees of the Constitution." Indeed, if in the United States "there was one-half the real love of liberty" present in Haiti, "everyone of their national representatives who voted for that infamous bill would be tried for his life, condemned and publicly executed as an accessory to man stealing." Holly hoped to rally black support for the emigration movement. He felt that few efforts had been made to "vindicate" Negro character with the result "that many of the race themselves are almost persuaded that they are a breed of inferior beings." He announced that instead of "proving Negro equality, I should prove Negro superiority." And he ended by pointing out the advantages of Haiti as a home for the continued advancement of the Negro nationality.[18]

Holly made one point quite clear amidst the rhetorical flourishes and specious logic that threatened to overwhelm the subject matter. The United States did not want him or any other free Negro. In the eyes of most whites a Negro was not a desirable member of the community, especially if he refused to exist in a state of subordination. Holly considered it better to build up a black nationality in Haiti than to remain in the United States where, even if political rights were granted, "a social proscription stronger than conventional legislation would ever render them nugatory."[19]

In November 1855 the foreign committee denied Holly's application for a missionary appointment to Haiti. His importunities seemed to have irritated the members of the committee, especially the Reverend Gregory T. Bedell, who reacted unfavorably to Holly's news that money from the treasury of the board of missions would have to be spent to launch a successful mission in Haiti. The committee was not only $10,000 in debt, but it also had severe misgivings about the capabilities of all Negro missionaries. They had just heard at a previous meeting a long report on the condition of the Liberian mission with all its hardships and "extra" expenses of "lumber shipped in, supplies shipped in, indolent native workers, bad climate, and only three of our missionaries working with the heathen, the rest with colored emigrants." These problems only reaffirmed what the committee had long suspected about the inadequacies of black churchmen—they should never be allowed to work without white supervision and they should be paid considerably less than their white counterparts.[20]

Rebuffed by the foreign committee the still-rootless Holly gratefully accepted the rectorship of a black Episcopal church in New Haven. Emigration plans would have to wait.

## III

Less than six months after he had received deacon's orders in Michigan, Holly was ordained a priest on January 2, 1856, by John Williams, the assistant bishop of Connecticut. He had once more used his intelligence to win for himself in Williams a new and influential white friend. As Williams remembered it long afterward, when Holly presented himself to the bishop and a board of clergymen for his canonical examinations, the bishop, taking into account his lack of formal education, offered to be lenient in the Greek and Hebrew exams. Holly replied: "I could not respect myself if I did not pass all the required examinations." He then easily did just that.[21]

St. Luke's Episcopal Church, where Holly entered upon his duties as rector in December 1855, had been organized formally in 1844 by a separation from its white parent, Trinity Episcopal Church. The first minister, the Reverend Eli Stokes, a Negro, went to Liberia as a missionary and his successors, when any could be supported, had all been white. Although a small church, St. Luke's was now to serve as Holly's base for the propagation of Christianity and emigration.[22]

Holly, whose one-year appointment would be stretched into five, proved to be a popular figure in the black community. The half-dozen black clergymen in New Haven normally ranked among the elite of the city's 1,500 Negroes, and Holly was no exception. He found himself in constant demand as a speaker at Negro social events, including convocations, suppers, and Masonic meetings. He also practiced a very active ministry, conducting services on Wednesday evenings and Sundays, and officiating at baptisms, marriages, and burials. As rector he exercised strict control over his growing congregation, readily admonishing parishioners who were delinquent in tithing or tardy to worship services. Under his leadership St. Luke's remained in relatively good financial condition during a period of nationwide economic uncertainty. True, his own salary was often in arrears, but over $300 was raised to improve the church edifice.[23]

Four months after moving to New Haven Holly certified, and probably wrote, a call, issued over the signature of William C. Munroe, for a second national emigration convention. The convention was to be held in Cleveland in August 1856. Once again, prospective delegates were warned that only emigration to North or South America would be discussed. This limitation reflected Holly's fear that advocates of African emigration would seize control of the meeting.[24]

Throughout the summer weeks prior to the convention Holly absented himself from New Haven to lecture in the Eastern and Midwestern United States and Canada. On this tour he alternated his fiery and nationalistic "Vindication of the Capacity of the Negro Race for Self Government" with a more moderate discussion of the religious needs of Haiti. He addressed the former lecture to black audiences and the latter to Sunday school classes of white Episcopalians. According to a white reporter, Holly's spoken delivery was "clear, earnest and eloquent." A Negro observer praised his "gentlemanly appearance and his mellow voice . . . precise manners . . . interesting and eloquent preaching."[25]

Frederick Douglass and other antiemigrationists virtually ignored the "Call" to the August meeting. Indeed, the only newspaper that promoted the convention was the *Provincial Freeman,* directed by its outspoken editor, Mary A. Shadd Carey. Mrs. Carey, who had in the past been highly critical of Holly and decried all emigration except that to Canada, now urged "all who can to go to Cleveland and determine to remove to a country or countries where you may have equal rights." When the convention met it was sparsely attended. Holly and his friends, Munroe, Whitfield, and John P. Anthony of New Haven and St. Luke's Episcopal Church, directed the proceedings in the absence of Martin R. Delany, past president of the national board of commissioners and now a practicing physician in Chatham, Canada West, who remained at home ill. Delany's influence prevailed, however; he was reelected president and Chatham was selected as the site for the next meeting in 1858.[26]

Several projects emerged during the sessions. Reminiscent of the defunct North American League in 1851 was a proposal to create a North American and West Indies Trading Association as "the basis of a fixed and definite policy among our race." Stock was to be sold for $50 a share, and the funds therefrom invested in the West Indies trade by an official board of trade. Free blacks would thus be able to invest their money in an organization competing directly with the slaveholding sugar and cotton growers of the Southern United States. As in the case of the League in 1851, however, nothing ever came of the Trading Association plan.[27]

The delegates in Cleveland revived another project of Holly's left over from the convention in 1854, the *Africo-American Quarterly Repository.* This journal "of the Literature, Art and Science of our race" was to be written, edited, and published for Negroes by Negroes, with Whitfield as senior editor and Holly, Delany, Munroe, Mary Bibb, and Mary Shadd Carey among the corresponding editors. Before the senior editor could authorize publication, one-thousand advance subscriptions had to be sold. They were not forthcoming, and the journal failed to materialize.[28]

Moreover Holly suffered disappointment in regard to Haiti. Although he recounted to the convention the results of his trip the previous year, he could not produce solid guarantees of support from the government of Haiti; and the convention refrained from singling out the Black Republic as a preferred site for colonization. Interest in the West Indies in general was reaffirmed, however, and Holly was elected foreign secretary of the national board of commissioners. As secretary he would write letters "in every direction, among which were several states of Central and South America, as well as Jamaica and Cuba."[29]

By now it was evident to Holly that the national emigration board and its conventions were not a practical means of promoting emigration to Haiti. Martin R. Delany, president of the board, had become increasingly enamored of African colonization, and a "quiet conservatism" had settled over the organization. But Holly's activities at the conventions of 1854 and 1856, his voluminous correspondence on behalf of the movement, and his lectures, published letters, and statements had propelled him to prominence among his brethren. Holly had become an independent force within an ever-diversified emigration movement. His growing reputation, coupled with increasing maturity and a boundless energy, would enable him to find new approaches and new allies.

"I am not opposed," wrote Holly to Martin R. Delany, "to pressing white men
into our service so long as they fulfill the behests of our race. The Anglo Saxon
now predominates in this country because he presses all other races into his service. It will be mere folly and madness in us to refuse to do the same. I do not care
for the persons of men so long as the cause of our race is subserved." Thus Holly
answered Negro associates who criticized him for working with and through
whites. Like his associates, he scoffed at the rhetoric of white superiority, and he
too preached black supremacy. But he was realistic enough to know that American blacks by their efforts alone had in the middle of the nineteenth century neither the funds nor the impetus to achieve a Negro nationality. The Haitian emigration movement needed white allies.[1]

**I**

In New Haven children attended segregated schools. When Holly arrived in that
city it supported three "colored" schools, including the ungraded Whiting Street
Grammar School under the direction of Ebenezer Bassett. In 1856 Bassett moved
to Philadelphia, and the Whiting Street School was closed. In the autumn of 1857
the school reopened and Holly was offered the position of principal. He served
in that capacity until summer 1859, when the newly created board of education
closed the school to blacks and ordered it "refitted" for white scholars. Little is
known about Holly's success as a public school teacher in New Haven, but Daniel
Coit Gilman, official visitor in 1858 and later president of Johns Hopkins University, reported the best spelling in town in Holly's school.[2]

Holly opened his own private institution in the summer of 1858, the New Haven
Select School for Young Colored Ladies and Gentlemen. The four-year curriculum
included daily Episcopal devotionals and a strong emphasis on race pride. The
achievements of Liberia and Haiti, "the only two acknowledged Negro governments in the world," were stressed. The school offered its graduates a unique cer-
tificate of "Preceptor of Common English," which Holly, prone to exaggeration,
called "something special for New Haven Negroes."[3]

Holly was now serving as a parish priest, teaching and delivering lectures for the emigration movement, but he somehow found time to prepare a manuscript on Masonic ritual that appeared as a series of articles entitled "A Compendium of the Fundamental Principles of Intermasonic Comity" in the *American Freemason* from July 1858 to June 1859. The editor of the journal found that Holly's undertaking, which amounted to a treatise on proposed changes in Masonic law, "possessed the merit of originality to furnish evidence that their author is a scholar, and a man of no ordinary ability." When the skin color of this "scholar" became known, Southern Masons indignantly denied Holly's right to be a Mason or to contribute to Masonic periodicals. The *American Freemason* replied that the magazine did not judge a man by his antecedents, caste, or color.[4]

Between 1856 and 1859 Holly attempted to develop new support for Haitian emigration. In July 1856 he and William C. Munroe created an organization grandly titled the Convocation of the Protestant Episcopal Society for Promoting the Extension of the Church Among Colored People. This body and its association for women, the Society of the Sisterhood of Good Angels, had two functions, to recruit American blacks into the Episcopal church and to solicit aid for their eventual emigration to Haiti. In the Black Republic the emigrants would assist in restoring the island's Catholic worship "to its primitive purity."[5]

Holly was genuinely interested in the recruitment of American blacks into the church and the field was in a sense almost limitless. The Anglican communion had been in America as long as the English and there had been a formal Episcopal church in the United States since 1784, yet three-quarters of a century later Holly could find only seven Negro Episcopal congregations served by four priests and one deacon. Total Negro membership barely reached 300 and could not be expected to increase very rapidly considering the dearth of trained black clergy and the general hostility shown the Negro by white churchmen. Led by Southern slaveholders and Northerners such as Bishop Hopkins, the church did not hesitate to brand blacks as unfit for the responsibilities of freedom and innately inferior in every way to the white man. Thus there appeared to be little future for Negro Episcopalians in the United States. What Holly wanted from white churchmen was financial aid to enable him and other Negroes of like religious belief to emigrate.[6]

The Convocation of the Protestant Episcopal Society for Promoting the Extension of the Church Among Colored People produced few substantial achievements. The Society's cofounder and president, William C. Munroe, became discouraged at the failure of his own congregation in Detroit to grow, and he lost his teaching position in that city when Negro opponents of emigration successfully petitioned for his dismissal. In 1858 Munroe moved to Brooklyn and once more requested the foreign committee of the Domestic and Foreign Missionary Society to send him, with or without his friend Holly, as a missionary to Haiti. Denied this appointment, he shifted his interests from the Caribbean to Africa. Holly must have been pained at this defection and he experienced more frustration from other members of the Society. Samuel V. Berry, who replaced Munroe as president, gradually became opposed to Haitian emigration. When Holly finally managed to emigrate to the Black Republic, only twelve members of the Society followed him.[7]

## II

Holly was convinced by the late 1850s that free Negroes, working strictly on their own, could not successfully accomplish a mass emigration project. As a serious student of past emigration ventures, he realized that the American Colonization Society would have foundered without the help of public white men. While it was true that the Society's success had been sporadic, over 5,000 American Negroes had been transported to Liberia. Holly hoped that socially and politically influential white Americans, especially men active in the national government, would be brought to support Haitian emigration. He reacted promptly and favorably when, in January 1859 Congressman Francis Preston Blair, Jr., of Missouri, a firm believer in the incompatibility of the races, presented a plan to provide the free black population of the United States with homes in Central America. As Blair envisioned it, these Negroes would establish themselves as a free and independent people under the patronage and protection of the United States.[8]

Holly immediately wrote to Blair to solicit his support for emigration to Haiti. Receiving a favorable response, he sent the congressman a lengthy second letter in which he answered Blair's questions about the results of the convention movement and the interests of black Americans in colonization. Holly reported with his typical rhetorical flourish that

> even the convention organization in its extent is but a feeble expression of the growing feelings of discontent at their anomalous condition in this country now rife among free blacks, both North and South. Many are not identified with this movement, because they look upon the effort to remove and colonize themselves as wholly impracticable without the helping hand of men of power, influence and wealth of this country.... They have looked upon this organization of their people as a fond Utopia, to be dreamed of, but never to be realized. ... But now that your speech in Congress opens a new era in their hopes ... I can assure you that thousands can be readily enrolled as emigrants to the intertropical regions of our continent with the slightest effort.... I am confident that with proper inducements to be held out before them in regard to security for liberty, property and prospects for well doing, I could muster two-hundred emigrant families, or about one-thousand free colored persons, annually, for the next five years, of the very

best class for colonial settlement and industry, from various parts of the United States and Canada, who will gladly embark for homes in our American tropics. At the end of this period, because it would regulate itself thereafter . . . like an electric spark, a spontaneous emigration, double that of the first, will follow in the second five years, and this number will be trebled or quadrupled in the succeeding decade.

The early success of Blair's colonization project, Holly continued, might cause the United States government to support the enterprise. Yet Holly was realistic enough to understand that Blair's "opportune agitation" in Congress was "all that I believe can be done for years to come with our government on this subject." The practical details of launching an emigration project must be carried by "private individuals of influence, character and standing throughout the whole country." This type of help was not forthcoming. Frank Blair, his brother Montgomery, and James Doolittle, senator from Wisconsin, undertook a round of speechmaking to seek white support for the movement. But other political obligations and interests soon sidetracked them.[9]

Although Holly's efforts to establish a black Christian nationality in Haiti consumed most of his time and energy, he remained active in the life of the Negro community of New Haven. In the spring of 1859 he led a group of Negroes to protest against the discriminatory policies of the board of education. Speaking as both a parent and a teacher, he contended that the inadequate education offered free blacks in the Northern United States helped ingrain social and racial injustice. The public schools for Negroes in New Haven—physically inadequate, understaffed, and not accessible to all black children—proffered a second-rate education to second-class citizens. While the schools for whites improved yearly, the institutions for blacks foundered. After the protest the New Haven Board of Education sought to correct some of the deficiencies of the Negro schools by the "easy" step of replacing all the black teachers with whites. This action, according to Holly, implied that "colored teachers are incompetent." Although he now ran his own private school, he organized a group of sixty Negro heads of families who petitioned the board of education to reverse its decision and to improve the physical plant of black schools. The petition criticized the board for removing the black teachers and thereby breaking "that ultimate social sympathy" between Negro instructors and their black pupils. The point was well taken because many Negro families in the antebellum North were fragmented and lacked stability. A regular black teacher, in Holly's opinion, offered an element of permanence to Negro children. In response, the board of education pointed out that properly qualified "colored" teachers were hard to come by, and continued to hire whites. Nevertheless, physical conditions in the Negro schools of New Haven were gradually improved.[10]

Holly, hoping to reach an audience broader than that represented by black Episcopalians, found time during spring 1859 to prepare a series of short articles entitled "Thoughts on Hayti" that were published in the *Anglo-African Magazine*. These pieces presented his views on the condition of American Negroes and the future of the Republic of Haiti. In great measure he repeated the theme of his earlier *Vindication of the Negro Race—* namely, that Haiti represented the destiny of the black people. He admitted the disadvantages under which the Black Republic labored: erratic leadership, the "corrupted forms" of Romanism, and the indifference of the "powerful and enlightened nations of the world." However Haiti could achieve national regeneration under her new leaders, though the society was "sadly deficient in the elements of morality and industry." Negroes from the United States were needed to supply the mission with religion, industry, and education. In other words, Holly's recruits and religion would help solve the problem.[11]

Holly continued to seek help from Episcopal missionary officials, achieving some success in the autumn of 1859 when Gregory T. Bedell, the assistant bishop of Ohio, agreed to mention Haiti's claim in a sermon before the annual meeting of the board of missions. Encouraged by the reception of Bedell's sermon, Holly again applied to the foreign committee for a formal missionary appointment to Haiti. Through the aid of the retired bishop of Constantinople, Horatio Southgate, now a prominent New York clergyman, he was able to submit documents in support of his proposal. In them he pointed out that within the preceding year over 500 American Negroes had left New Orleans to settle in Haiti, that many free blacks in Florida planned to emigrate, and that a colonization group in the nation's capital boasted a common treasury of $3,000. Officers of other missionary societies with whom he had talked told him that the new president of Haiti, Fabre Geffrard, welcomed all Protestant missionaries.[12]

Once again the foreign committee declined to support a missionary in Haiti. The committee's formal answer to Holly pleaded financial difficulty, but the confidential minutes reveal that the committee thought Haiti was too small, too divided, too uneasy politically, and too lacking in governmental control and in influential commercial relations to warrant support. By contrast, the committee had the previous year approved the opening of new missions to Japan and Brazil on the ground that they showed "evidence of being great countries of influence."[13]

Undeterred by this failure, Holly unfolded a new plan. After conferring with Thomas Brownell of Connecticut, the presiding bishop of the church, and John Williams, the assistant bishop of Connecticut, he decided to try to establish a church in Port-au-Prince, Haiti, under the immediate supervision of Brownell. This mission would be supported by the individual contributions of the Episcopal laity with some aid from Anglicans in Great Britain. In the spring of 1860 Holly wrote to Leonidas Polk of Louisiana asking that Polk, as the bishop nearest Haiti, visit the island yearly once the mission had been established. Considering that Polk had been a large planter and was still a slaveholder, it appears that Holly would go to any lengths to achieve his goal.[14]

Shrugging aside financial difficulties, Holly single-mindedly pursued his dream of emigrating to Haiti. He had long struggled with poverty; in 1860 he owned no real estate, and the value of his personal property was listed at $100. Yet he refused a call, with guaranteed salary, to the rectorship of St. Philip's Episcopal Church in New York City—the richest, most prestigious, and largest Negro church in the United States. He had long before reviewed the Negro's chances for a future in America and found none. When he moved again it would be to Haiti and not New York City.[15]

By the autumn of 1860 Holly had abandoned his school teaching. Most Sundays his pulpit at St. Luke's remained empty while he traveled the countryside preaching the merits of the Black Republic. He instructed prospective emigrants among his congregation to occupy themselves in his absence studying French, the national language of Haiti. If invited to address a meeting of church women, he would speak of the need for industrious church women in Haiti. If called, as he often was, to serve as a grand instructor of the Masonic organization, he always managed, after the formal installations, to speak on the advantages of life in Haiti. In declining an invitation to address a commemorative meeting for the martyred John Brown, he managed to argue for emigration. His brethren, he said, had to learn from Brown's error not to rely upon the "insurrectionary manhood of the enslaved and dehumanized portion of the race in the active work of their own regeneration." Instead, he argued, the free blacks in the United States should remove themselves to Haiti. The result would "tell in the speedy disenthrallment of America."[16]

## III

Before the Blair business lost its momentum and his last application for a formal missionary appointment was denied, Holly discovered new friends in the emigration movement. First of all, the emperor of Haiti, Faustin Soulouque I, a "brutal, ignorant worshipper of snakes and hater of intelligence," was overthrown in 1858 by General Geffrard, optimistically described as a "gentleman of fine talent, culture . . . the foremost Haitian of the age." And then Holly found a young Scottish journalist and abolitionist, James Redpath.[17]

Redpath, a born agitator and reformer, first reached prominence in America for his accounts of John Brown's activities in Kansas. He then took an extended tour of the Southern states, wrote three books, and conducted three reporting trips to Haiti. A combination of circumstances and events, including his visits to the Black Republic, his empathy for American Negroes, and his own need to be active, landed him in the middle of the black emigration movement. He had not always been sure of his commitment. In May 1859 he warned Frederick Douglass that American Negroes should not emigrate to Haiti until President Geffrard had given written assurances of his government's intentions. By the autumn of that year Geffrard had promised that (1) land would be available on long-term credit in all parts of the country; (2) his government would advance money to pay the passage of all emigrants of two- or three-hundred families if desired; (3) American Negroes would live together in communities of two- or three-hundred families if desired; and (4) the government would allow complete religious freedom to non-Catholics, citizenship after one year, and exemption from military service for seven years. These guarantees literally duplicated the demands Holly had made of Soulouque's regime in 1855.[18]

The Haitian government followed up its promises by appointing Redpath the Haitian commissioner of emigration in the United States. His annual budget of $20,000 included a personal salary of $5,000. In Holly's view, Redpath had "reaped the first fruits of Holly's mission." He attributed his own failure to receive the appointment to having unavoidably broken his vow of 1855 to return to Haiti the next year. He believed, however, that the Geffrard government had placed upon Redpath the "express injunction that Rev. Holly should be called to cooperate with him." And when Redpath returned from Haiti in the early fall of 1860, he did offer Holly a salary of $1,000 plus traveling expenses to engage emigrants for Haiti. Thankful for the opportunity "to prove my devotion to the Haitian government," Holly accepted. At last he would be able to guarantee financial help to prospective emigrants.[19]

Holly now committed himself to a definite date of departure for Haiti. In November 1860 he mailed a circular entitled "The Establishment of the Church in Hayti" to all Episcopal church publications and bishops. In it he announced that he would sail the following May and that "it is a settled point on my part . . . to go at any sacrifice to establish a church in Hayti." He predicted that his mission would be self-supporting after five years from stateside Episcopalians.[20]

The greatest boon to Holly's personal efforts and Redpath's Bureau was an increase in the acceptability of the idea of colonization by American blacks. Both Martin R. Delany and Henry Highland Garnet, the latter a past opponent of emigration, were championing movements to Africa. Frederick Douglass, the most influential of American Negroes at this time, had insisted as recently as 1859 that "upon no consideration do we . . . favor any schemes of colonization," but was now prepared to join the emigrationists. He admitted in print that "whatever the future may have in store for us, it seems plain that the inducements offered to the colored man to remain are few, feeble and uncertain." Douglass had met privately with Redpath and was attracted to Haiti as the logical place for emigration. His reasoning paraphrased Holly's arguments of the 1850s: "It seems to me that it would be . . . little advantage to slavery to have the intelligence and energy of the free colored all concentrated in the Gulf of Mexico." Douglass, like Holly, rejected emigration to Africa. "Let him [the Negro] remember that a home, a country, a nationality are all attainable this side of Liberia."[21]

Many blacks, however, still disliked the idea of emigration to Haiti and denounced Redpath and all connected with his Bureau. Delany, now an advocate of African colonization, berated Holly for working with a white man. Holly defended Redpath's "tried faithfulness to the cause of the race" and jestingly blamed Delany's ill temper and inconsistency "on some fetish trick, learned perhaps from some savage tribe in the jungles of Central Africa."[22]

The most effective Negro critic of the Haitian emigration movement was James McCune Smith. A native of New York City, Smith had studied medicine in Scotland after being denied admission to schools in the United States. By 1860 he owned two drug stores and much real estate in the Negro areas of New York City. Smith had always believed emigration to be a poor solution for America's racial ills, and he now had obvious business reasons for opposing an exodus of Negroes. Through his influence the New York *Anglo-African,* a newspaper owned by Thomas Hamilton, shifted from modest support of emigration to strong opposition, publishing pages of criticism directed at Redpath, Holly, and their new associate, Henry Highland Garnet. Editor Hamilton also delayed printing Holly's responses for weeks at a time.[23]

A battle broke out between the Smith (or New York) "clique," and Holly and Garnet as emigration agents. Smith charged that "the master Redpath" was deluding prospective colonists, and that Redpath and Holly were covering up the details of the unsuccessful emigration of American Negroes to Haiti in 1824. Was Holly traveling in behalf of "negro nationality or negro rascality"? In his rebuttal Holly opened with his usual hyperbole:

> I have an utter aversion to touch or handle anything emanating from the crafty and insidious spirits which borrow for themselves a fancied greatness because they happen to have been born in and about the city of New York. Speaking from . . . experience . . . that city is the Sodom and Gomorrah of our race in America and the would-be-great men therein I do not desire to touch with a 40-foot pole.

Yet Holly could not allow Smith's "treasonable designs against the race" to go unanswered. Admittedly, the emigration in 1824 had been a failure, but it was deficient "self-reliance" among the emigrants that doomed the project, not any lack of effort on the part of the government of Haiti. Smith responded by daring the enthusiastic Holly to "answer me directly! don't scare up a stump to whack me around . . . don't let the words run away with you. Try and think a little. . . . Throw the adjectives overboard." Garnet and Holly, Smith insinuated, were involved in the emigration movement only for the salaries they received from Redpath.[24]

Because much of Smith's criticism was right on target, Redpath moved to eliminate the problem of the "Smith clique" by using funds from the government of Haiti to buy Hamilton's paper outright. Now it was Smith's turn to be denied access to the "communications" page of the newspaper. With the *Anglo-African* safely in Redpath's pocket, Holly's panegyrics concerning Haiti filled each issue of the journal and its successor, the *Pine and Palm*.[25]

Holly had been recruiting emigrants since the end of November 1860 in Pennsylvania, New Jersey, and New England. He was instrumental in filling up most of the second shipload of emigrants sent off to Haiti on January 2, 1861. His activities in the Philadelphia region were effective enough to attract the attention of William Coppinger, secretary of the American Colonization Society. In November 1860 Coppinger reported to a friend that "I doubt if a corporal's guard can be got off from this region." Four weeks later he wrote that "the Haytian Movement appears to have made considerable headway in this city."[26]

Holly and his fellow recruiting agents, including John Brown, Jr., son of the martyr of Harper's Ferry, Garnet, J. B. Smith, William Welles Brown, H. Ford Douglass, and William J. Watkins, worked up a regular schedule of appearances in their assigned areas. They usually spent one day in each small town and several in the metropolitan centers. Their audiences were normally composed of Negroes, although on occasion some whites interrupted the meetings to bemoan the possible loss of their "valuable workers." After a quick sketch of Haiti's history that downplayed the political instability, the speaker would extol the beauties of the island. A list of potential colonizers was drawn up, after which each prospect received an individual visit from the agent, who was required to check into the personal character and habits of those who wished to have their expenses paid by the Haitian government.[27]

Holly set up certain standards he expected emigrants to meet. Foremost was "manly self-reliance." He looked for "unobtrusive, industrious, peaceable, intelligent, moral, progressive and useful citizens." In other words, "they should not be like the Irish." He wanted no shirkers like the "rabble" that had gone to Haiti in 1824 and "wilted away" in their new home because "they longed for the fleshpots, the leeks, the onions, and the garlic of domestic servility in the United States." Every emigrant needed to be his own employer and to develop his own vocation—

not seeking office and emolument but content to be "industrial Civilizers" developing the natural resources and wealth of Haiti. The goal for Haiti was *"not simply a negro nationality but a strong, powerful, and enlightened and progressive negro nationality, equal to the demands of the nineteenth century, and capable of commanding the respect of all the nations of the earth."*[28]

Working as an agent under James Redpath did not prove to be easy. Redpath continually voiced suspicions concerning the qualifications of his associates, especially when they questioned his management. His way was the right way, and he had a ready answer for all his critics. He blamed the opposition of most Negro clergy upon their fear of losing their congregations. Any hesitation by prospective emigrants was attributed to the false propaganda of the American Colonization Society or the "New York clique." He never accepted any blame for the Bureau's failures, but passed it on to his workers in the United States and Haiti. His letters to the Haitian government at times reflected a veiled contempt for American blacks and seem almost paranoid in their accusations of the "treacherous and falsehearted" men working for the Haitian Emigration Bureau.

In public Redpath praised all his agents. But scorn for his black coworkers appears in his correspondence. For example, when too many emigrants arrived to board a ship in New York City and extra costs were incurred, the blame was laid to "a want of business tact on the part of Mr. Holly." After the recruiting of emigrants began to fall off with the outbreak of the American Civil War, Spanish unrest in Haiti's neighbor, Dominica, and the news of disease and death in Haiti itself, Redpath again faulted his agents. In reporting to August Elie, general director of emigration to Haiti, he lamented that he had never been able to secure "first-class men." He found his American associates, "Holly, William Welles Brown, William J. Watkins, H. Ford Douglass, J. B. Smith . . . only of the second class." He described Frederick Douglass, whose support he had sought with some success in December 1860, as "amiable" but "easily bought." When Douglass later changed his position, Redpath compared him to the character in *Pilgrim's Progress* called "Mr. Facing-both-ways."[29]

Beginning in early 1861 Holly concentrated his efforts as a Bureau agent largely in the New Haven area. His main concern was his own "New Haven Pioneer Company of Haytian Emigrants." For them he issued detailed rules and instructions on March 1, 1961. The group of "not more than fifty families" would be settled in one body on a "magnificent estate," the property of President Geffrard, three miles outside Port-au-Prince. The company would cultivate the estate "in shares" for three years. At the same time each member would select and begin to improve a grant of government land for his future home. Holly's instructions emphasized that he sought not to stifle individual freedom but only to ensure "mutual cooperation, protection and help as good neighbors."[30]

The departure of the New Haven colony was threatened by the eruption of fighting in both the United States and in the Dominican portion of the island of Haiti. News of the Spanish government's attempt to reassert control over the Dominicans upset many prospective colonists. Holly tried to allay the fears of his people and was able to write to Redpath that "none of his New Haven colony would remain [in the United States] in consequence of the recent news from St. Domingo." His last-minute efforts on behalf of the Bureau in Philadelphia were less successful. There he found a failure of leadership among the city's Negroes that he attributed to their "latent dehumanized manhood." Like Redpath, Holly refused to lay any blame on himself or the idea of Haitian emigration.[31]

The New Haven colony, originally projected to sail on April 24, did not finally embark for Haiti until May 2, 1861. The outbreak of hostilities at Fort Sumter forced Redpath to consider that an American ship "full of free Northern colored men would be a splendid prize" for the Confederacy. Hence a British ship was substituted. She touched at Boston, where the Haitian Emigration Bureau had its headquarters, to take aboard fifty-two passengers as well as "nervously worn out" Redpath, then proceeded to New Haven. There, after a resounding "Farewell Meeting" attended by a large crowd, both white and black, Holly and his New Haven colony, 101 members strong, boarded the *Madeira* and sailed for Haiti.[32]

**V**

**The
Battle
for
Survival**

Haiti has changed little in the last 150 years. The Haiti of Geffrard that James Theodore Holly encountered in 1861 was much like the Haiti of Dessalines in 1804 and that of "Baby Doc" Duvalier in 1978. This slowness to change can be largely traced to the country's geography.

Located 1,400 miles directly south of New York, the Republic of Haiti occupies the western third of the Caribbean island that Columbus called Española, sharing it with the Dominican Republic. Though small, Haiti is impressive in terrain. An English admiral, when asked by George III for a description, crumpled a sheet of paper and threw it on the table. Haiti is a land of rugged mountains, plateaus, narrow, isolated valleys, and coastal plains. The step ranges that rise along the coast crisscross in the interior, making internal communication difficult and restricting the marketing of agricultural and industrial goods mainly to the seaboard. These same mountains have always encouraged sectionalism, fostered division between city and countryside, weakened national government, and sheltered insurrectionists.[1]

Haiti had inherited no "white problem" upon winning independence after a bloody struggle with France in 1804. The whites who had not been killed fled the country. Haiti inherited instead a different type of race problem. When the slave revolt erupted in 1791, approximately 30,000 freedmen, the light-skinned offspring of French planters, lived in Haiti. Humiliated by the discrimination that separated them from the white community, these freedmen united with the slaves in the final overthrow of the French. After the birth of the Haitian Republic, however, they constituted a mulatto elite that jealously guarded its property rights and superior social status. The blacks, 95 percent of the population, tilled small farms. The elite, who dominated the professions and civil service, made it a rule not to engage in manual labor. Yet Haitian law, unlike that of the United States, never legitimized any racial distinction. The unwritten law proved sufficient. Much of the history of Haiti has been colored by the struggle between these two groups. The military remained one of the few institutions not directly dominated by the elite. Through military influence Haiti was ruled by a succession of black presidents, many of whom were corrupt, semiliterate generals.[2]

Although Haiti was generally regarded as a French-speaking country, French was understood and used by only 10 percent of the people. The national language was, and still is, Creole, a version of the old Norman-French of the seventeenth-century buccaneers spoken with the accent of African slaves. The elite remained partial to French culture and adhered tenaciously to the French language and the Roman Catholic faith. In contrast, the illiterate black masses spoke the dialect and practiced the Vodun, or Voodoo, folk religion of their African ancestors, combined with a bastard type of Romanism. These blacks married without formal ceremony, practiced polygamy, and remained isolated from the outside world.

James Theodore Holly and his fellow emigrants to Haiti faced these domestic obstacles as well as the ever-rising criticism directed at them by antiemigrationists in the United States. Within weeks Holly's hopes for a black Christian nationality were crippled by desertion from his ranks and by the disease and death that spread through the colony

I

Holly exercised great influence over the *Madeira's* shipload of emigrants. He required each member of his group to sign "solemnly stipulated articles of agreement." In obvious emulation of the pilgrims, the signers of the "*Madeira* Compact" pledged that they would "seek less to advance our temporal interest than to labor for the establishment of the Kingdom of God in Hayti." Holly said, "No other colony of men ever came to Hayti with such a high and holy purpose. Hence Satan never had so much to fear."[3]

The colony consisted of thirty-seven recruits from Connecticut and sixty-four from Massachusetts, New York, Pennsylvania, and Canada West. The ship also carried fifty-seven colonists bound for the port of St. Marc. This additional group produced such overcrowding, despite the hiring of another vessel to carry baggage, that only after Redpath bribed the customs officer was the *Madeira* allowed to clear the port of New Haven and sail for Haiti.[4]

Upset already by a full week's delay in sailing, many on the *Madeira* became even more discouraged with the routine fare—beans, salt pork, and hardtack—and with the seamanship of their captain. The usual passage of ten to twelve days to Haiti was stretched to twenty-nine by unfavorable weather. The ship was first blown off course, with high seas causing considerable seasickness among the passengers. Then she was becalmed for nearly a week off the island of Tortuga before finally disembarking a portion of her passengers at St. Marc, Haiti. Arrival at Port-au-Prince on June 1, 1861 brought only more annoyances and delays. The fumbling of Haitian customs officers and the insufficient wharf facilities required the emigrants to be disembarked in shallow boats and rafts. In the confusion Holly's wife, Charlotte, was swept into the sea and nearly drowned.[5]

Once the colonists were ashore the situation temporarily brightened. Despite the primitive surroundings and grumblings usual among strangers in a foreign land, the experience of living under a government ruled by men of their own color and of seeing black officers command black troops thrilled the new arrivals. As one emigrant wrote home, "I am a *man* in Hayti where I feel as I never felt before, entirely free." Another found Port-au-Prince, for all its "dark and dingy appearance,"

> to me the most enchanting city I have ever visited for *it is the capital of the Negro Republic* which has demonstrated the wisdom and progress of our race. As I walked the streets of the capital I felt as no colored man in the United States can feel. I beheld her Senators and Representatives, her judges and her generals with admiration and respect.[6]

Soon after he had disembarked, Holly hurried to the National Palace to present to President Geffrard his letters of introduction from Redpath, B. C. Clark, the Haitian consul in Boston, and his diocesan bishop, John Williams of Connecticut. Williams's was a letter of dismissal addressed to President Geffrard because there was no Episcopal bishop in Haiti. It praised Holly, honorably dismissed from the Diocese of Connecticut, and placed him in Geffrard's hands. According to Holly, Williams's letter "opened the door for the Episcopal Church in Haiti." A few days later Holly led a delegation of his colonists to present the president with a carved chair brought from the United States. The third meeting with Geffrard took place two weeks after the *Madeira*'s arrival for the purpose of baptizing a child born on the passage out. Holly performed the service at the National Palace in "halting" French and the president of Haiti stood as godfather to the infant.[7]

Holly's colonists had all taken an oath of allegiance to the Republic of Haiti and pledged to become citizens. Even so, they were obliged to remain in Port-au-Prince at the emigration depot while temporary living quarters were being built at their future home, Drouillard, the former estate of a wealthy French family that Geffrard had occupied after he became president. Holly and Geffrard hoped that successful farming by industrious American Negroes would demonstrate to the Haitian people the importance of agriculture and stimulate the growth of other such projects throughout the country.[8]

The New Haven colony had arrived during the rainy season when one day might see five or six thunderstorms and almost as many inches of rain. The three weeks to be spent at the emigration depot became six, and the original enthusiasm of many colonists began to fade. There were illnesses, fatalities, and then desertions. By the time the company moved to Drouillard in mid-July 1861, refugees from the Holly compound had arrived back in the United States, where their appearance was greeted with delight by the recently revived *Anglo-African*. This antiemigrationist paper reported widespread fever among the emigrants in Haiti and commented on the backwardness of the Black Republic.[9]

The *Anglo-African*'s remarks contained much truth. Holly's colony did indeed appear to be in danger of disintegrating around him. The elderly and the young children were the first to perish, falling prey to the "acclimating fevers" brought on by the downpours, the intense tropical sun, crowded quarters, and impure water. Fevers raged uncontrolled through the poorly ventilated shed, 300 feet in length, that housed all the colony. Holly's elderly mother Jane and his young daughter Cora were early fatalities. Another was John P. Anthony of New Haven, a zealous advocate of Haiti. His death deprived Holly of his staunchest friend and most dependable coworker.[10]

Holly nevertheless continued to hold his colony together. He cajoled them into staying, stressing that he had repeatedly warned of possible difficulties and that the pilgrims had also experienced hardships in 1620. He compared health conditions for Negroes in New Haven with those of Drouillard and found Drouillard better. When colonists protested that Haitians washed, bathed, and drank from the same stream, he reminded them that the Negro areas of New Haven had no drainage; tainted soil; raw sewage in the streams; pigs and cows in the streets; endemic dysentery, typhoid, and malaria; and a death rate twice that of whites. He discounted the recent deaths, including those within his own family, telling the emigrants that his first two children, Anna and Ella, "all we had," died of a fever in 1856 three weeks after he had moved to New Haven.[11]

Two events that shook Haiti in July 1861 caused a temporary cohesion of the colonists. The colonists were incensed when supporters of the ousted dictator, Faustin Soulouque I, threatened to overthrow President Geffrard. Geffrard had taken a special interest in the New Haven colony, visited it regularly, entertained Holly, and provided food, ice, and nurses for the colony's sick. Consequently, when his administration was endangered the emigrants rallied to the support of the president. The second event involved a fleet from Spain that was sent to the island in response to the unrest and attacks on Spanish citizens in neighboring Santo Domingo. Because of Haiti's alleged aid to the Dominican rebels, the Spanish anchored in the Port-au-Prince harbor and threatened to bombard the city. The able-bodied men of the New Haven colony again pledged their support to their adopted land, and Holly agreed with the Haitian authorities to arm his men at Drouillard in expectation of a land invasion by the Spanish.[12]

The end of the threat against Haiti by an outside force and an increase in typhus at Drouillard brought about another drop in morale. By early September fourteen members of the colony had left Haiti. Among them was the widow of Holly's friend William C. Munroe. She had informed readers of the *Anglo-African* that "you would not want to live here. I am coming home as soon as I can." Holly, himself a victim of typhus, announced from his sickbed that the deaths sustained were a "triumphant witness in behalf of the noble cause of Haitian emigration." This tactless remark brought a published rebuke from James Redpath, who was frantically writing the Haitian government to stop all emigrants from returning to the United States. Redpath correctly surmised that desertion could be the death-blow to his languishing Haitian Emigration Bureau.[13]

Opponents of Redpath's Bureau seized upon the news of disasters in Haiti as an excuse to step up their campaign against emigration. The *Anglo-African* led the way. Denunciations and denials from Holly succeeded only in magnifying the debate. When Holly called for "stouthearted emigrationists . . . friends of a colored nationality who are not afraid to die," the *Anglo-African* observed that it was true that Haitian heat decomposed matter more rapidly than in Connecticut. "But it does seem a queer way to build up a 'colored nationality' by enriching a soil." The paper also played up rumors that Mrs. Holly had gone insane and that Holly himself, "disheartened and disgusted, had left Port-au-Prince and gone to California."[14]

Holly refused to let the controversy die. In a letter to *Pine and Palm* he denounced both the deserters "who had left their post of duty" and "the servile character of free colored people of the United States." Nineteen members of his colony had died, he admitted, but the rest at Drouillard were convalescent, and farm work had commenced. Lecturing his "soulless" brethren in the United States who had spread false rumors about "my family," he confessed his shame for all black Americans "because they are afraid to die like independent, self-respecting freemen. . . . Hence their greatest argument against Haitian emigration turns upon this cowardly fear." Holly, a man who rarely tolerated criticism, also had harsh words for a deserter who had dared to criticize his leadership: "Whoever this asinine creature is, I regard him as a vagabond scribbler."[15]

In New Haven Holly's letters aroused organized opposition against his colony and their leader. A prominent white minister, J. Kenady, sought to discourage further emigration to Haiti, announcing that he had been denied permission by the Haitian government to charter a ship to bring back emigrants who wanted to leave Haiti. Holly's friend and successor at St. Luke's Church, Samuel V. Berry, believed the "misguided" Holly to be "reckless, overbearing and domineering." The Negroes of New Haven were upset with Holly and his letters, which Berry called "the most foul and slanderous upon the colored people of this state ever known." An assembly at St. Luke's, with Berry as chairman, voted that all persons connected with the "infamous scheme" of emigration were the "real enemies of the Negro in America." In a more moderate tone, Berry recommended that Holly "leave off wrath" and "lay aside all bitterness." Many in the United States would sympathize with him if he would let them. "But your sweeping denunciations against us stifle the sympathy of your warmest friends." Berry ended with a warning: "Let not the impulse of misdirected zeal destroy you."[16]

Despite the increasing criticism leveled at Haitian emigration, there still remained pockets of support for the movement. Friends of Holly in New York City organized a "New York colony" that planned to settle in Haiti on land adjoining Drouillard, but it never did so. The writer of a letter to *Pine and Palm* wanted to join Holly to "promote the glorious cause of colonization and Christianity." A black Episcopalian vowed to go to a place where the church contained "no negro pew." Nevertheless, no new emigrants joined Holly's colony.[17]

Hard pressed simply to hold his colony together, Holly now chose to ignore his critics. He seemed never to rest. He tilled his garden, made and repaired boots and shoes, preached on Sundays, cut up and distributed beef and ice provided by the government, cooked, and nursed the sick. On Christmas morning 1861, his wife Charlotte died after an illness of three months. Six days later his infant son, Joseph Geffrard, was buried, the forty-third member of his colony to be "laid low in the dust." Deeply grieved, Holly pledged that he and his two surviving sons, Augustine and Theodore Faustin, "would remain until the time of our sacrificial offering." He wrote his friends in New Haven that "Hayti is dearer to me now than ever, because here repose the ashes of those nearest and dearest to me."[18]

With the worst epidemics passed, Holly concentrated his efforts on making Drouillard a successful agricultural operation. He soon discovered that items essential for the "inauguration of a new era of industry," such as a sawmill or a plank road to connect Drouillard with the capital, never materialized. Holly's colony was able, however, to clear thirty acres of primeval forest and plant cotton and vegetables. In late March 1862 Henry Melrose, an agent sent by Redpath, visited Drouillard and reported that Holly "had no regrets" and considered prospects in Haiti "encouraging." Holly himself was in excellent spirits and planning to visit the States in the autumn to sell the cotton crop. He did intimate to Melrose, however, that the New Haven colony might eventually abandon the estate and its unhealthy location.[19]

## II

Holly had during the first year in Haiti little time for evangelical work among the "unenlightened." The Episcopal services held on Sundays at Drouillard attracted some native onlookers, but the onslaught of sickness and the desertion of Holly's hand-picked assistant, the Reverend R. R. Morris, temporarily halted most scheduled worship. Yet Holly still held firmly to the goal he had pledged himself to on his first day in Haiti: "that our arrival . . . might be indicative of the conversion of the people of this island from the errors of Romanism to the pure scriptural and Catholic truths of the Reformed Church of Christ."[20]

By mid-1862 Holly's dream of a successful mass emigration of American Negroes had failed. He must have realized as much. The threat of military disturbances in Haiti, the failure of the Haitian government to provide promised land, and the reports of sickness and death among colonists in locations all over the island had discouraged the flow of emigrants. Clearly, Haiti was not the promised paradise. But to Holly the tragedies, a work of Satan—"the mysterious power of the air"— only strengthened his resolve. He perceived the deaths in his own family as "a baptism of fire" and understood them to be God's way of testing him.[21]

He had to now throw all his efforts behind the regeneration and purification of the Black Republic through the establishment of a branch of the Episcopal church in Haiti. He knew exactly what he wanted to accomplish and how he would accomplish it. He needed to be subsidized by funds from abroad. From the expected donations he promised to build a national Episcopal church with its roots in the Anglican community, yet independent in its own right. This Anglican-Episcopal offspring, the first national Christian church of any kind in Haiti, would need the direction of its own bishop. He had to be a black, a man filled with spiritual zeal, an enthusiastic lover of his race. Holly could think of only one man supremely qualified for the job.

The only hope of securing immediate aid was a return to the United States to launch an appeal in person to the foreign committee or, better yet, to the general convention, which would meet in October 1862. After the United States, Holly dreamed of going to England to appeal for funds through the influence of the Lord Bishop of Oxford, Samuel Wilberforce.[22]

Holly sailed for the United States early in September 1862, leaving his two young sons behind in the care of the colony "as a guarantee of my return to Hayti and to assure them I would not desert them." Holly spent the month before the general convention calling on prominent East Coast clergymen. No evidence survives to show how he was received by the Negro community during his stay in New York and New Haven, but the passage of the best part of a year since the protest meeting in New Haven, as well as the failure of Redpath's emigration plans, may have soothed the rancor.[23]

Holly took with him to the United States the promise of a rent-free hall in Port-au-Prince for church services. Now he had to secure a missionary stipend. His first efforts failed miserably. At the time when he was seeking an appropriation for Haiti, the foreign committee was recalling missionaries from abroad and cutting back expenses. In debt $15,000 from the previous year, the committee had, in January 1862, issued an "urgent call" for the "exercise of prudence and of wise forethought to guard against going beyond the point which the Church would sustain." It was not surprising, therefore, that Holly's pleas met a series of rejections. The foreign committee first buried his request in a subcommittee and then flatly refused to give him a stipend. His memorial to the general convention, asking for a missionary bishop "to oversee the spiritual interests of Hayti" and payment of clergy and teachers for a five-year period, fared no better. Wrapped up in debate over the problem of churchmen in the Confederacy, the convention had neither time nor interest for Holly and Haiti. The presiding bishop routinely assigned Holly's memorial to the care of a committee of three bishops, Alonzo Potter of Pennsylvania, Carelton Chase of New Hampshire, and George Burgess of Maine, and asked them to report at the next general convention—in 1865.[24]

Holly, although most comfortable by practice and belief with the high, more ritualistic wing of the church, now turned to an infant Episcopal missionary group, the American Church Missionary Society. The Society, founded in 1860 and composed of low, or evangelical, churchmen, resented that although low-church parishes contributed the greatest amount of support for missionary work, the new missionary bishoprics and dioceses had nearly always fallen to the more ritualistic churchmen. The American Church Missionary Society wanted a ministry of "evangelical, spiritual men" whose interests lay in the "saving of the souls of their fellow men." Their sphere was to be the whole domestic missionary field beyond the organized dioceses. Foreign missionary fields had not been mentioned, but this did not prevent Holly from soliciting their support for his church in Haiti.[25]

Shortly before his return to Haiti Holly received, through the influence of two New York clergymen, Heman Dyer and Stephen Tyng, a hearing before the executive committee of the American Church Missionary Society. Impressed with his plans to evangelize the island and to "introduce a strong Anglo-Saxon element into Hayti by the purifying effect of the Episcopal Church," the Society granted Holly $150, promised him future aid, and declared Haiti to be a "singularly providential opening for missionary efforts." It would be another two years before the Society acknowledged to its rival, the foreign committee of the board of missions, its intention to enter the work in Haiti, but Holly had received enough encouragement to go home in high spirits.[26]

Early in 1863 the Society applied to the presiding bishop of the church, Thomas C. Brownell of Connecticut, for guidance in regard to Haiti. Brownell then appointed Bishop Alfred Lee of Delaware to undertake an episcopal visit to Haiti "to ascertain the condition of these people." Besides the promise of Lee's visit, Holly, though not officially designated a "regular missionary," began receiving a monthly appropriation of $50.[27]

Two immediate changes faced Holly upon his return to the Drouillard plantation in November 1962: a marriage and a relocation. He married the woman he had left in charge of his sons, the former Sarah Henley of New Haven, a devoted churchwoman who had come to Haiti with Holly's colony. Continued habitation at Drouillard was by now impracticable. Periodic sieges of fever and the general failure of the agricultural experiment forced the twenty remaining colonists to move to the capital at the end of 1862. Holly, although financially pressed, refused an offer from the Haitian government to relocate in the city of Aux Cayes as a professor of English at the lycée with a salary of $600 in gold and a rent-free residence. He would abandon neither the remnants of his colony nor his plans for a national church of Haiti with headquarters in Port-au-Prince.[28]

Both spiritual and practical reasons drew him to Port-au-Prince. He believed that he had been called to preach the Kingdom of God in Haiti, "commencing at the capital, as the apostles did beginning in the great cities of the nations." On the more mundane side, Port-au-Prince was attractive to Holly because it dominated the political, economic, intellectual, and social activities of the Republic.[29]

Living in Port-au-Prince had its drawbacks, to be sure. The highest cost of living on the island was to be found in the city of 30,000 inhabitants, where "New York City" prices must be paid from meager Haitian wages. Holly's monthly salary from the American Church Missionary Society, sent to him in depreciated United States greenbacks, did not meet all his expenses. He lived in a "miserable hovel surrounded with mud and water and filled with humidity," and he supplemented his income by teaching English to private students. Even so, he began to slip into debt. But his church work went on. The move to the capital increased the size of his congregation. In July 1863 Holy Trinity Church was organized and formally acknowledged by Presiding Bishop Brownell as a parish under the jurisdiction of the general convention of the Protestant Episcopal Church of the United States. And in November 1863 the long-awaited visitation and inspection by Bishop Lee took place.[30]

Accompanied by the Reverend C. H. Williamson, who spoke French, Lee spent three weeks in Haiti. Holly spared no effort in trying to impress the bishop with the importance of church work in Haiti. In Port-au-Prince he arranged for Lee to stay in the mansion of an American merchant and to have interviews with the president of Haiti, the minister of public worship, and the American consul. In the course of his visit Lee confirmed twenty-six candidates in church membership, and he and Williamson preached to large native audiences.[31]

Lee returned to the States "very favorably impressed" with Holly, his labors, and his "zeal, prudence, perseverance and remarkable energy." He reported "gross moral darkness" in the island and asked the Society to act at once because "the gospel is the only effective way to elevate a people." He did not share Holly's sanguine belief that the mission in Port-au-Prince, given proper financing, would be self-sufficient in five years. But Holly's ideas were evident in Lee's statement that "a convenient and appropriate church is a sine qua non, and accommodations for schools and a residence, for one missionary at least, is of the first importance." The missionary in Haiti, he said, should be paid in gold and supplied with prayer-books, hymnals, and tracts in French. Lee warned the Society not to expect the mission to be exempt from difficulties, discouragements, and hindrances.[32]

Holly's euphoria at the success of Lee's visit did not last. Troubled by the uncertainties of the Civil War, the Society declined to follow Lee's recommendation that it adopt Haiti as a new missionary field. It did agree, however, to keep Holly on salary and to issue an appeal for $15,000 for church buildings in Port-au-Prince. Holly continued to receive the same basic message from Heman Dyer, corresponding secretary of the Society: "Everything is so unsettled in our country that we cannot form any definite plans. You must, therefore, feel your way along and be as patient as possible."[33]

In Haiti unsettled political affairs were endemic. Holly's five decades there would see frequent changes of president and wholesale destruction of property. In July 1863 President Geffrard was able to announce that the fifth attempt to overthrow his government had failed, but exactly two years later another revolution erupted in the northern end of the country, bringing repercussions to all parts of Haiti. Prices soared, particularly in the capital, where all foodstuffs doubled. Holly's landlady demanded that he repair his house at his own expense or face a raise in rent. These difficulties came at a time when his family had been increased by the birth of his second child in two years. Holly's income had been reduced to one-third of its former amount because his English students had been forced to give up their studies. To avoid abandoning his ministry he was forced to draw, without authorization, a three-month advance on his salary. This necessity of going into debt and borrowing on his salary was to him "the bitterest cup that I have yet been called upon to taste in this field."[34]

News from the United States was no brighter. Bishop Alonzo Potter of Pennsylvania, long a supporter of the American Negro, had promised to visit Haiti to acknowledge Holly's formal appointment as the only foreign missionary of the American Church Missionary Society. But his trip was prevented, first by his illness, then by news of an outbreak of yellow fever in Haiti, and finally by his sudden death. After Potter the Society turned to Bishop George Burgess of Maine. Although only lukewarm in his support of the Society, Burgess accepted the call. His journey to Haiti was scheduled for early in the summer of 1865, but was postponed when revolution broke out in the Black Republic.[35]

Along with news of the delay of Bishop Burgess, Holly learned that the Society's efforts to raise money for Haiti had not been successful. More discouraging still was a notice in November 1865 that jurisdiction over Haiti had, "in the interest of greater harmony," been transferred from the American Church Missionary

Society to the foreign committee of the board of missions. The foreign committee had in the past refused to help Holly. He wrote to the secretary to the committee, Samuel Denison, to reintroduce the mission and to reiterate the hope of the American Church Missionary Society that the change would make it possible for the mission "to work in a more efficient manner." Denison's reply not only exhibited a general lack of understanding of the economic situation in Haiti, but it also sternly rebuked Holly for his overdrafts on the American Church Missionary Society. Holly was stung by the criticism and complained bitterly of "this wound." He detailed his humble condition: only one substantial meal a day, "quite shabby" dress, and a hovel for a home. His best hope for the survival of his mission now lay in the visit of Bishop George Burgess.[36]

# VI

# The Continuing Struggle

In 1921 an American Negro newspaper, the *Church Advocate,* assessed the life of James Theodore Holly in an editorial. It linked Holly with Frederick Douglass and found that "both men wrought well and courageously in their day and generation." The nineteenth century had been a time, the *Advocate* supposed, "when a Negro could obtain most anything in reason in the shape of honors, were he willing to lead the way to Africa or Haiti." Unfortunately, it was never this easy for Holly.[1]

## I

George Burgess, bishop of Maine, was a dying man when he accepted the invitation of the foreign committee to visit Haiti. A veteran of nearly thirty-two years in the ministry, Burgess now chose to end his days in a foreign mission field. He and his wife spent two weeks vacationing in Cuba, St. Thomas, and Barbados on the way to Cape Haitien, the former center of French culture in Haiti, where they arrived March 5, 1866. Here they expected to be met by St. Denis Bauduy, a Haitian-born, English-educated mulatto, who for twenty-five years was a Wesleyan minister in Haiti (Holly had recruited him to serve as an Episcipal missionary at Cape Haitien), and by Holly himself. But the first Haitian steamer Holly and Bauduy boarded at Port-au-Prince sprang a leak and was compelled to turn back; and the second was in such poor condition that Holly and Bauduy were a week late in meeting Burgess.[2]

At Cape Haitien Holly preached and Burgess ordained Bauduy to the Order of Deacons. This service was disturbed by the din of a nearby court-martial of revolutionaries who had failed in a recent attempt to overthrow the Geffrard government. The ensuing executions, in which 200 shots were fired to kill six men, caused Burgess extreme discomfort. Presently he, his wife, Holly, and Bauduy departed for the capital on a warship as guests of the Haitian government.[3]

Arriving in Port-au-Prince "weary and jaded" after two sleepless nights on the crowded ship, Burgess spent his first day witnessing a "tremendous calamity."

The city was burning, and the pattern of the fire was all too typical of such tragedies in the capital city of Haiti:

> All the morning the land breeze blew, and wafted the raging flame, which
> swallowed everything in its path, and widened its path on both sides. There
> was nothing like effective resistance; generally none at all; goods were re-
> moved but the houses went down like stubble. There were no engines of
> any force . . . no organization . . . no real leadership. So the conflagration
> swept out of existence all that broad, best part of town which covered the
> plains toward the edge of the sea; and when this was exhausted, the wind
> also lulled, and the dreadful work seemed over. But at this crisis all the resi-
> dents said that when the sea-breeze should spring up in an hour or two
> later, it must waft the flames back upon its track and towards other parts of
> the city still uninjured. Was anything then done, attempted, proposed, or
> encouraged? Nothing; and the whole people waited in silence or in noise
> the coming of the sea-breeze which carried the flame past where it was ex-
> pected; and having rolled and roared over streets and squares, made its path
> up the hill, and in the evening died for lack of fuel. Oh what a mournful day
> for those who were wealthy, and in a few hours had not a change of raiment!
> What a tremendous blow to the city, the nation, all trade, all credit, all con-
> fidence! I was told that half the city of Port-au-Prince was no more.[4]

Holly had removed his furniture and papers from his rented house when the
flames approached. The fire spared the house but consumed the hall where his
church services were held. Holly's personal situation was now distressing, his rent
being past due and his impoverished parishioners, suffering from stagnant trade
and spiraling prices, in no position to do anything for him.[5]

Burgess's visit in Port-au-Prince, which stretched from March 19 until April 22,
impressed him favorably with opportunities for preaching the gospel in Haiti.
He wrote Secretary Denison that he agreed with Holly's plan to extend the church
work out of the city into the mountains of Leogane, where it would attract the
simple country people. The foreign committee should grant formal missionary
appointments to Bauduy and to Julian Alexandre, another of Holly's recruits to
the ministry, and place the Haitian mission on a "liberal foundation" by supplying
Holly with a new house, a new church, and a suitable salary. Lack of enthusiasm
on the committee and a real shortage of funds prevented Burgess's suggestions
from being carried out. Holly did receive, however, a salary increase of $900 per
annum.[6]

Bishop Burgess's health had continued to decline while he labored alongside Holly,
and he died on shipboard exactly twenty-four hours after departing Port-au-Prince.
His last words were incoherent mumblings about the needs of Haiti. Though his

death deprived Holly of an influential supporter, it did stimulate his friends in the American church to give money enough not only to build a memorial church and school house in Port-au-Prince, but also to enable Holly to send three Haitian youths to be educated in the United States for missionary work in Haiti.[7]

Holly's selection of the first boy for this purpose brought on a minor quarrel with the foreign committee. The captain on whose ship the boy, Pierre E. Jones, traveled to the United States reported to Secretary Denison that he was listless, dull, and unintelligent. The foreign committee was shocked to find him only one step removed from Roman Catholicism. Presently Bishop Lee criticized Holly for "acting inconsiderately" in dispatching such an ignorant Haitian to America. In response, Holly was quick to tax his superiors in the United States with errors and lack of Christian understanding in the case. The seeming "dullness" of the boy Holly blamed upon the boy's seasickness, his inability to speak English, his absence of companions, and his fear of the wickedness he expected to find in the United States. Jones had heard that to abduct people to use in their experiments medical students employed hotel beds that dropped their occupants down a chute to the eager anatomists. Fearing robbery Jones carried his purse in his boot, making him limp. In time Holly would be powerfully vindicated, for this boy whom Secretary Denison and Bishop Lee wanted to send back to Haiti as hopeless became the first Negro graduate of the Episcopal Seminary in Philadelphia and returned to Haiti to work as a missionary and professor well into the twentieth century. The history of this particular episode typified, both in the hasty conclusions drawn in the United States and in Holly's indignant replies, the misunderstandings between Holly and his fellow workers in Haiti on one hand, and churchmen in the United States on the other.[8]

Perhaps the greatest difference of opinion in the long relationship between Holly and American church authorities arose over Holly's attempt to lay down rules for the church in Haiti. His extreme high-church proclivities and his exalted view of his own authority clashed sharply with the low-church views among the bishops concerned and with their narrow interpretation of Holly's authority.

When Holly had proposed to organize a convocation of missionaries in Haiti, Bishops Lee and Burgess assented. But Lee had understood that the convocation would be simply an "organization for missionary purposes"—that is, a social and religious gathering of workers in the field, and not the equivalent of a stateside diocesan convention where church legislation could be considered. What Holly actually did was publish, early in 1868, a *Registre de la Convocation* setting forth a major body of rules and doctrines. Upon receiving the *Registre* Lee was outraged to find that Holly, "as chief actor," had established and approved his own exposition of the catechism and Christian doctrine. Among the offensive articles was the statement that "the catechism used by the Pastor of Holy Trinity Church,

Port-au-Prince must be the model for all other parishes in Haiti." The *Registre* also decreed that any other changes made by the dean of liturgic prayer were to "be adopted for use." And all this had been accomplished without a word of consultation with the American church or with Lee, the overseeing bishop for Haiti. Holly, as pastor of Holy Trinity and dean of liturgic prayer, was clearly bent upon setting up his own religious empire in Haiti.[9]

The *Registre de la Convocation* also contained much exaggerated doctrine and many articles objectionable to authorities in the American church. It was high-church heresy, and written by a Negro. Bishop Lee disliked Holly's genuflection to the Roman Church, especially the call for "respect always for work already done by Romans." The low-church members of the foreign committee objected strongly to Holly's support of baptismal regeneration—the belief in an instantaneous moral change in the recipient of baptism. "Mr. Holly has undertaken to do what none of our bishops and Diocesan Conventions would have dreamed of doing. That such views should be identified with the missionary work of our church . . . appears . . . deplorable." They ordered the *Registre,* with its "extravagance and error in doctrinal statements," withdrawn from circulation. Rebuked for his "unwarranted actions," Holly was warned that "so long as he acts as a missionary of this Committee he must be obedient to their wishes."[10]

As was to be expected, Holly's reply sought to justify his actions. In a "spiritual" defense, he explained to Bishop Lee that, since the Protestant Episcopal church had taken permanent root in Haiti, "tangible and definite information in regard to the Anglican communion" was needed for prospective churchmen. Denying all doctrine "not found upon the positive teaching of the word of God," Holly declared that he was an "Evangelical Christian" who "clung to the word of God pure and simple." In a lengthy "moral" defense he justified the rules and regulations of his *Registre* on the ground that he was teaching "moral lessons" to the Haitians. Because of their revolutionary tradition, strict guidelines must be laid down for them.[11]

Not impressed with either defense, Lee forwarded Holly's letter to the acting foreign secretary, William Morrell, with the judgment that the excuses were unsatisfactory even if one made allowances for Holly's "vanity and self-esteem" and his desire "to appear great and learned in the eyes of his countrymen." Lee suggested sending Holly books that might help "disabuse his mind of the sacramutations [*sic*] he has imbibed."[12]

Holly made some effort to resist the foreign committee's decrees. To John Henry Hopkins, presiding bishop of the church at this time and the man having "primary jurisdiction over my work," he protested in March 1868 that "the screws have been put in to make me cease to proclaim the full gospel here." Low churchmen, "perhaps well intentioned, but with rationalistic tendencies," were taking over the American church and applying a censorship similar to Rome's "cast-iron system." This letter went unanswered, Hopkins having died. Arthur C. Coxe, bishop of western New York, another old friend of Holly, apparently cautioned him to obey the foreign committee and to bide his time. This advice meant only one thing to Holly: to wait until he became bishop of Haiti. He did promise Coxe to "impose silence upon myself," and he kept busy with parochial missionary work in Port-au-Prince, directing the erection of a new church and conducting thrice-weekly study sessions with his candidates for Holy Orders. Only occasionally did he forget his promise and protest bitterly to Secretary Denison the suppression of his annual convocation. His complaints were ignored.[13]

Conscious of the increasing formality and coldness in the letters he received from the foreign secretary, Holly went over the heads of Lee and the foreign committee and addressed a request to the new presiding bishop, Benjamin Smith of Kentucky. He asked for the means to pay the full support for five missionary clergy, to endow a seminary, and to provide a bishop for Haiti. Smith's reply, cosigned by Alfred Lee, acknowledged that the Protestant Episcopal church owed "a vast debt to the African race," but suggested that the most imperative claim was that of the four-million freedmen in the United States.[14]

Given permission by Bishop Smith to solicit aid from the Anglican church, Holly began a correspondence with individuals in England and with two English missionary groups, the Society for the Propagation of the Gospel (SPG), and the Christian Knowledge Society (CKS). A correspondent for the CKS advised Holly to have his old diocesan bishop, John Williams of Connecticut, appeal directly to Samuel Wilberforce, the bishop of Oxford. Besides this suggestion, which came to naught, Holly received enough favorable responses from Britain to encourage him to project a trip there in the summer of 1870. But Bishop Lee and the foreign committee not only refused to grant travel funds but actively discouraged the journey. In a letter to Secretary Denison, Lee remarked that Holly would no doubt "be well received and awaken a good deal of interest in his mission but he would be likely to fall into the hands of extreme High Churchmen and come back more than ever imbued with that spirit." After having refused to increase missionary funds for Haiti, the foreign committee now would not allow Holly to raise funds for himself. Their opposition to the trip, combined with his own ever-present poverty, quashed the proposal.[15]

## II

Both the mission family and property in Port-au-Prince frequently fell victim to political incendiaries. Part of Holly's problem was that his church and rectory were on a lot, donated by President Geffrard in 1866, which was only one block from the government arsenal. When the arsenal was sabotaged in November 1866, the Holly family escaped unhurt, but the blast blew out all their windows, overturned their furniture, and bent double the half-inch iron bars on their front door. In 1868 the Episcopal Mission of the Holy Comforter and the entire suburb of Bel Air were destroyed in a fire started on orders of the new Haitian president, Salnave, who hoped thereby to squelch opposition to his dictatorial regime. A year later a bombardment of the arsenal from the nearby harbor forced Holly to remove his family to the mountains. Then in 1873 a successful assault on the arsenal set off a citywide fire that engulfed Holly's church, school, and rectory.[16]

Despite the uncertain political climate Holly believed that if the work of preaching the gospel did not move forward aggressively in Haiti, it would not merely stand still, but would move backwards. The number of lay readers, catechists, and candidates for Holy Orders grew during Holly's first decade in Haiti, but the total number of ordinary converts to Episcopalianism was small. Visits by Holly and his assistants from door-to-door in Port-au-Prince brought few responses. Most urban citizens were at least nominal Roman Catholics and indifferent to Protestantism. Funds were too limited for Holly's mission to offer inducements of social services, such as trade schools or medical clinics. Even so, new parishes— very small ones—were gradually established in Cabaret, Cape Haitien, Aux Cayes, Jacmel, and Jeremie, and the work continued to flourish among the peasants in the mountains of Leogane.[17]

A significant handicap to the work of the mission in Haiti was the long interval (April 1866 to December 1872) between the second and third episcopal visitations. Only a bishop could ordain a postulant for Holy Orders into the diaconate, or a deacon into the priesthood. Thus for a six-year period Holly and Bauduy remained the only two priests, and only they could administer communion because deacons could not officiate in that sacrament. Ostensibly, the principal reason for the long delay in finding an American bishop to visit Haiti was that none could spare two months from his own diocese. Another obvious reason was the peril that might be encountered on such a visit. Bishop Burgess's last voyage and death had been well narrated in church newspapers, and notices of revolution, yellow fever, and typhoid outbreaks in Haiti were commonplace in the lay press. Besides that, few churchmen or their bishops felt any affection for or obligation toward the Negro in Haiti. If Negroes were to receive medical, education, and spiritual aid, then this support should go to the recently freed Southern slaves in the United States or to the "true heathen" in Africa.[18]

A series of bishops—Burgess's brother-in-law, Bishop Kip of California; the retired missionary bishop of Liberia, John Payne; Bishop John Williams of Connecticut; Bishop Alfred Lee of Delaware; Bishop Henry Washington Lee of Iowa; Bishop Clark of Rhode Island; and Bishop Whipple of Minnesota—all declined to visit Haiti. Holly blamed this reluctance not upon the reasons suggested here, but upon his old scapegoat, "the Prince of the Power of the Air." His setbacks came not from "the follies of mortal flesh and blood" but from the "invisible ruler of darkness." It was "Satan, the Arch Rebel" who had profited by the cancellation of convocations, the revocation of the *Registre,* and the postponement of episcopal visitations.[19]

## III

The selection of two presidents, one in Haiti in 1867 and the other in the United States the following year, had a direct influence on Holly's life. The Haitian voting robbed him of a friend, slowed his church work, and increased his financial difficulties. The election in the United States reunited him with a friend and brought him prestige and more financial stability than he had known before in Haiti.

The election of Sylvain Salnave to the presidency of Haiti in May 1867 brought civil strife to the Republic and severe financial hardship to many of its citizens. Riding the crest of "conspiracy and rebellion—the blackest crimes of Satan," as Holly put it, Salnave had maneuvered his own election after a coup d'etat that forced Holly's friend and patron, President Fabre Geffrard, to flee the Republic. Within a few months much of the countryside was in insurrection. In April 1868 Salnave decreed himself president for life, thereby signaling the start of civil war all over Haiti. The American minister-resident in Port-au-Prince, C. H. Hollister, wrote Secretary of State Seward in May that rebellion raged at St. Marc, Aux Cayes, Gonaives, and Jacmel. Port-au-Prince was in a constant state of disturbance and "not safe for anyone to go out after dark."[20]

Soon Hollister wrote that the "condition of the city is growing worse." Salnave had already burned thirty homes and threatened to destroy the entire city unless it proclaimed its support of him. When the city acquiesced to his demand, it came under siege by Salnave's opponents. In August Hollister reported that "the state of things here are truly terrible—the poor people are suffering beyond what I can tell you of, commercial interests are nearly destroyed." Holly wrote Denison of his disgust at Salnave and the president's mulatto supporters, the woeful state of his own finances, the runaway inflation, and the standstill in all church work.[21]

On June 29, 1869, while civil war still raged in Haiti, a new American minister-resident arrived in Port-au-Prince. Ebenezer Don Carlos Bassett, Grant's appointee, was the first American Negro diplomat ever sent to a foreign post. He was also an old friend of James Theodore Holly. Bassett's trip to Haiti had been "exceedingly disagreeable," made so both by seasickness and by a brief view of wartorn Cape Haitien. He wrote his friend and mentor, Frederick Douglass, that the sight of people "in an absolutely starving condition" upset him, along with the "chronic quarrels" referred to him by the American consul; and that the "jab-ber of French, Creole, Spanish, Italian, German etc. etc." created a "babel" in his ears, making him glad when they weighed anchor. On shipboard he was further appalled at the naked and seasick condition of the two-hundred refugees crowding the deck. When he reached Port-au-Prince Bassett was overwhelmed by a mob of people curious to see the Negro diplomat from the United States. It was a great relief, he wrote Douglass, when "our old friend Reverend J. T. Holly came to the rescue and took me to his house where I staid [*sic*] all night." But it was a long night of "hand to hand combat with an uncounted army of mosquitoes, bed-bugs and flying little gnats," and morning found him ready to take refuge in the mountains outside the capital.[22]

Although nobody's fool, Bassett needed help in wartorn Haiti, and Holly was his key. Indeed, Bassett had deliberately chosen Haiti over Liberia because in Haiti he would be able to draw upon Holly's knowledge and experience. Bassett insisted that Holly become his "unofficial" personal secretary at a stipend of $900 per annum. His sole duty, reported Holly, was to give Bassett "private and friendly information of use to him in his official position."

Holly for his part needed the extra salary. He had been unable during the current revolution to house, feed, clothe, and educate his six children on his missionary stipend of $900 a year, and the foreign committee had denied additional help. Hence, ignoring the disdain of his mulatto acquaintances, who considered manual labor demeaning, Holly had resumed his old vocation of shoemaking. Under these circumstances he eagerly accepted the post with Bassett, deeming it "not a whit more honorable . . . than shoemaking but perhaps less arduous and more congenial to my pastoral vocation."[23]

Holly was undoubtedly a great help to Bassett. As the honorary consul of the Liberian government in Port-au-Prince since 1864, Holly knew all the members of the diplomatic corps. As a friend of many representatives and senators, he was well attuned to the political events in Haiti and to the intricacies of its politics. Bassett spoke no French, and his instructions from Washington took weeks to reach him. "To carry him through," he had to rely on "common sense" and the advice of his friend Holly.[24]

Race conscious as he was, Holly had been overjoyed at the choice of Bassett, after three consecutive white appointees, to represent the United States in Haiti. He interpreted the event as a signal from God related to the Biblical prophecy of Negro advancement. Did not Psalms 68:31 tell the black man that "Princes shall come out of Egypt; Ethiopia shall soon stretch out her hand unto God"? To Holly it was imperative that Bassett's mission be successful. And he knew of no better way of ensuring that success than by service as the diplomat's "confidant" and personal secretary. Nearly all of Bassett's dispatches to Washington between his arrival in Haiti in May 1869 and mid-1871 are in Holly's handwriting. It is also obvious that many of the opinions on Haitian politics reported by Bassett came from Holly, especially the anti-Salnave sentiments and the call for a return to the law and order experienced under Geffrard.[25]

Relations between the United States and Haiti remained tense but peaceful throughout the twenty-eight months that Holly served Bassett. Holly was active in the work of the Mixed Commission on American Spoilation Claims, a body which in 1870–1871 examined the claims of American merchants against the Haitian government for losses sustained during the revolt against President Salnave. He also helped Bassett explain to Secretary of State Hamilton Fish the growth of anti-American feeling among Haitians. Holly and Bassett both blamed the attitude on President Grant's design to annex Haiti's neighbor, Santo Domingo. They advised against the annexation.[26]

Holly resigned his secretaryship in 1871 but continued to counsel Bassett and help make his ministry successful and popular with the government of Haiti. Holly was also a personal friend—in the beginning at least—of Bassett's successor, John Mercer Langston. And when Frederick Douglass served as the United States representative between 1889 and 1891, Holly again figured as an unofficial adviser. He was forever proud of his career as quasi-diplomat, and he apparently had a right to be. But his main ambition lay elsewhere.[27]

## IV

Holly's role as the confidant of the American Minister-Resident Ebenezer Bassett helped him win prestige not only in Haiti but also with his superiors in the Church Missions House in America. Initially, however, his acceptance of employment with Bassett almost terminated his connection with the parent church in the United States.

Early in September 1869 a wealthy black American expatriate, John Hepburn, a founder, senior warden, and substantial financial supporter of Holy Trinity Church in Port-au-Prince, sent Bishop Alfred Lee a list of charges against Holly. Hepburn's most telling accusation was that Holly's position as Bassett's personal secretary occupied "all or nearly all" his time. Except for Bauduy's missionary work at Cape Haitien, the Episcopal church in Haiti was standing still. Holly was also charged with ignoring the English-speaking members of his congregation in favor of native Haitians; with dictatorial practices that had prevented the calling of a vestry meeting for two years past; and with mismanagement of missionary funds.[28]

Lee, who was still upset at the affrontery of Holly's *Registre*, forwarded Hepburn's letter to Foreign Secretary Denison with the comment that Holly's diplomatic position as described by Hepburn, "a staunch friend of the mission from the start," was not justified. Holly "ought to have enough to do" in church work alone, and if he preferred "the remuneration of civil office to continuing a missionary of our Board" he should be removed in favor of Bauduy. After conferring with the foreign committee, Denison wrote Holly that his job as missionary was incompatible with his working for Bassett. One or the other had to be relinquished.[29]

Holly replied that he had at first refused Bassett's offer but had finally succumbed for two reasons, "the desire to be useful to him by every means in my power so that his mission might be an honorable and successful one," and the opportunity to supplement his income with a labor less arduous than shoemaking. The slanders of Hepburn, "a man from whom I indeed expected better things," Holly blamed on ambition and greed. According to Holly, Hepburn had wished to be vice-consul under Bassett and had hoped that Holly would use his influence to secure the job for Hepburn. But Holly had refused to compromise himself and had even turned down a bribe of $2,500 to intercede with Bassett on Hepburn's behalf. Denied the position, Hepburn swore "vengeance" on Holly. And now "I have the evidence," Holly grimly noted, "how well the barbed dart of malice can succeed in its evil designs even on *ex parte* testimony by your letter before me." Accompanying this reply to Denison was a highly complimentary letter from Bassett to the foreign committee praising Holly's race pride and the high esteem in which he was held among both American Negroes and the citizens of Haiti. Because of this "pride of race," Bassett continued, Holly "would have felt it his duty to give me without formal engagement and without compensation the very assistance he is now giving me."[30]

Bishop Lee and the foreign committee pronounced Holly's explanation and Bassett's defense "satisfactory." Lee thought that Bassett's association with Holly might have the good effect of preventing Holly "from being led away by the false theology which appeared to be attracting him." If Holly's duties at the American consulate replaced his shoemaking and did not interfere with his pastoral work "we can not properly object." Denison accordingly notified Holly that the committee were "disposed to allow existing arrangements to continue." Accompanying this permission, however, was a veiled threat that the "matter of religious interest and activity"—or, in other words, the number of converts—must increase because "calls are very urgent from other quarters and the question has been asked whether we shall continue the present effort in Haiti."[31]

Holly thus survived, with an admonition, a serious attempt to tarnish his reputation and halt the work of the church in Haiti. Not until the 1880s, after he was safely settled in the episcopate, would other, more scurrilous, attacks be made on his conduct.

# VII

## The Right Color

Twice during the 1870s the color of Holly's skin was to be an asset to him. His complexion ensured his election in 1874 as bishop of the Orthodox Apostolic Church in Haiti. And in 1878 the combination of his race and his elevated clerical position secured him a grand visit to the British Isles.

## I

James Theodore Holly had considered himself a potential bishop ever since he entered the Episcopal priesthood. In 1860 he had taken note of a statement by Bishop Benjamin Smith of Kentucky to the effect that "suitable men of dignity, prudence, equanimity and firmness ... with the requisite piety" to serve as bishop "can be found among our negro race."[1] A Southern moderate on the race issue, Bishop Smith regarded the black man as centuries behind the white man, but he recognized individual exceptions who were "pioneers in the civilization and Christian elevation of the black races." Among them were Holly's missionary friend, Alexander Crummell, and Holly himself.[2]

As early as 1862 Holly had petitioned the general convention for a bishop in Haiti. His ambitions stirred again in 1864 when he read in church newspapers of the effort of Alexander Crummell to change the status of the Liberian church from a mission under the Domestic and Foreign Missionary Society to an independent Protestant Episcopal church of Liberia. Holly congratulated Crummell, and, after urging him to ignore the "disparaging reflections cast upon him by the Foreign Committee," related his own plans to build an independent church in the Black Republic with himself as bishop. The Haitians needed a black man to lead a black church: "They want the real thing and no mere sham." Crummell needed to be on his guard when dealing with church officials in the United States because "we have not much to expect from white men." In the same letter Holly asked Crummell to help him secure from the college in Monrovia "a parchment of two D's because black men must hold up one another in this way." The honorary Doctor of Divinity degree would, Holly believed, boost his personal standing and prestige in the eyes of potential converts in Haiti and among status-conscious Episcopalians in the United States.[3]

In September of 1864, when his total church membership in Haiti was all of seventy-five, Holly asked a friend in the United States, the Reverend Arthur C. Coxe, to bypass the American Church Missionary Society and form a committee "to promote the establishment and support of an Episcopate of a branch of our Reformed Catholic Church in Haiti." Holly would be the ideal bishop, as he proceeded to explain:

> I am now a Haitian citizen, entitled to all the rights and immunities guaranteed to the same by the laws and constitution of my adopted country. I expect to live and die here; the heritage that I expect to leave my children is bound up with this first independent nation of my race. My political allegiance is to the government of this country. But my ecclesiastical allegiance is to the Church of another country. . . . In order to fight the Roman Catholics our first effort must be to raise up a national clergy with their own Bishop at their head so as to form a complete and integral branch of the Church Catholic within itself.[4]

The argument that Holly emphasized to Coxe he would continue to play up in all his future correspondence with stateside Episcopalians. In Haiti his black skin was not a liability, but an asset. Holly believed the blacks of Haiti were dissatisfied with the ministering of white Roman priests from France and Wesleyan preachers from England. They wanted a truly independent church for their Republic.

Holly had begun the formal organization of a church in Haiti with the establishment of Holy Trinity in Port-au-Prince in 1863. After securing a gradually increased appropriation from the United States and recruiting native clergy in Haiti, Holly made another move. In 1866 he established an annual convocation of Episcopalian missionaries in Haiti with a strict set of rules, the *Registre de Convocation*. Stateside opposition obliged him to give up the *Registre,* but he refused to alter his doctrinal beliefs. These he described as "no compromise of the truth, the word of God pure and simple." He discounted the organizations of the Baptists, Wesleyans, and African Methodists as ineffectual. Only the Protestant Episcopal church could outlast Romanism. But his proposed national church in Haiti had to have the episcopate, for to be without a bishop would be "like the play Hamlet with the part of Hamlet omitted."[5]

In March 1871 Holly wrote the foreign committee to request a three-month leave of absence to visit the United States that autumn. Ostensibly the purpose of his trip—the first to his native land in nine years—was to mend his second wife's ill health. Actually his primary reason was to attend the October meetings of the general convention of the Protestant Episcopal church so that he might renew acquaintanceships with the American clergy and press forward his plan for a national church in Haiti. His request for leave was approved by the foreign committee and its new secretary, William Hare.[6]

In June 1871 the annual Haitian convocation, meeting in Port-au-Prince under Holly's direction, drew up a memorial for him to present to the general convention asking that a bishop be elected for Haiti. Memorial in hand, Holly, his wife, and his newest recruit to the ministry, J. B. Quine, a former Roman Catholic priest, departed in late August for America. The Holly party had hoped to travel by steamship, but were forced by the niggardliness of the foreign committee to travel by sailing vessel. The committee was, to be sure, over $15,000 in debt, yet even the newest white missionary appointee still traveled by steamer. Negro missionaries, the committee obviously believed, could and should live on less salary, endure more hardships, and expect fewer comforts than their white counterparts.[7]

Arriving in Boston on September 4, 1871, the Hollys made a quick pilgrimage to New Haven to visit old friends. Holly then joined Quine in New York City, and the two men journeyed to the home of Bishop Alfred Lee in Wilmington, Delaware. Here, according to Holly, the Bishop "cordially welcomed" them and admitted Quine to the canonical exercise of the Episcopal ministry. Holly ventured alone to Philadelphia to visit the two young Haitian seminarians being supported there by Burgess memorial funds. Both in Philadelphia and in Baltimore, where the general convention met, he found a type of racial discrimination he had not experienced for nine years. In Philadelphia he was refused service at a bank, and in Baltimore he was allowed to attend meetings but not to sleep in a local hotel. Like all Negroes who used the Baltimore passenger railway, Holly stood in line for the one car in seven labeled "colored persons admitted to this car."[8]

The immediate gains from Holly's trip to the general convention of 1871 were slight. His memorial asking for a bishop was one of at least six similar requests. He was shuffled from committee to committee without result. Holly asked the retired missionary bishop of Liberia, John Payne, to make an episcopal visit to Haiti, but was rebuffed because, as he believed, Payne "felt a dread of us down here . . . and was not attracted toward our work here." Holly also felt, but did not say, that Payne, a native of Virginia, had "reservations" about the capabilities of all Negroes.[9]

On the other side of the ledger, Holly's interviews with Secretary Hare in Baltimore were a great success. Hare, soon to be elected a missionary bishop to the Indians of the Dakotas, exhibited warmth and understanding in his dealings with Holly. This in itself was a decided change from the cool and at times belligerent attitude that Secretary Samuel Denison had manifested toward Holly. Hare's successor as secretary in 1873, Richard B. Duane, would continue to exhibit the warmer, more Christian attitude characteristic of Hare.

Hare sent Holly back to Haiti in late October 1871 with the promise that an episcopal visitor to ordain deacons and confirm candidates for church membership would soon be forthcoming. But the secretary met repeated frustration in attempting to implement his promise. The bishops of Iowa, Ohio, Kentucky, and Minnesota all refused to go. Holly, who had six Haitian converts ready for ordination to the diaconate or priesthood, was bitterly disappointed and besieged the secretary with "voluminous" letters that detailed in urgent terms the need for a visitation. Out of fifty bishops in the United States, "could not one be found to come at any sacrifice to our rescue?" [10]

The complaint that most disturbed Hare was Holly's comparison of his own recruiting success in Haiti with the "inactivity" of the foreign committee and the American bishops. Holly sent Hare a list of all the prospective clergymen he had lost because they had tired of waiting for ordination and left Haiti or joined another denomination. Hare was also struck by Holly's historical analogy between the current state of the Haitian missionary field and that of the early Anglican church in the American colonies. Holly's argument was that other Protestant churches in America that performed their functions without bishops had prospered, whereas the Anglican church in the colonies, dependent upon the benefits of confirmation and ordination, had lost ground because of a shortage of native American clergy. It was a near miracle, he said, that he had been able to establish five organized congregations in the Black Republic. [11]

Secretary Hare did manage a certain number of positive measures to help the mission in Haiti. Through his efforts Arthur C. Coxe was appointed to replace Alfred Lee as the "overlooking" bishop for Haiti. Coxe, an old friend of Holly who shared his high-church tendencies, proved to be a forceful advocate of an episcopate for Haiti. He also squelched outright a letter sent to the foreign committee by one of Holly's parishioners in Port-au-Prince complaining about Holly's high-handed leadership. In addition, Hare secured dual appointments at $600 per annum for the recent seminary graduates, Pierre Jones and Charles Benedict, to return from Philadelphia and work in Haiti. They were to report to Holly as the senior missionary in Haiti and to follow his orders. Most important of all, the foreign committee in accordance with Hare's wishes honored Holly's request that he be appointed principal of the new parish school in Port-au-Prince. This job, originally intended for J. B. Quine, had fallen vacant after Quine's sudden death. The tuition received from scholars at the school enabled Holly to relinquish his job as personal secretary to the American minister-resident. [12]

## II

I have been into some of the wild regions of the plains near Port-au-Prince, where I felt myself, like Dr. Livingston, in the very heart of Africa. There were the same mud cottages, the same thatched dwellings of the black tribes just as you have seen presented in Dr. Livingston's travels. And from the dark entrances of these huts the naked creatures would look upon us, then dart away again, suggesting that they were simply savages. . . . For twelve miles I travelled through a deep forest almost impenetrable. . . . I was forcibly reminded of that wild dreary, wicked appearance which Dante gives to the *Inferno.*

This description of Holly's adopted land was written in 1872 by the Right Reverend Arthur C. Coxe, the first episcopal visitor to travel to the Black Republic since Bishop Burgess died off the coast six years earlier. Coxe, as "overseeing bishop," had taken upon himself the responsibility of visiting Haiti after no other American bishop could be persuaded to go. Twelve very rough days on a steamer brought him to Port-au-Prince on November 22, 1872. He had hoped to be back in New York for Christmas, but gave up this notion in favor of staying to do everything in his power to help Holly and the beleaguered Haitian Mission. He spent six weeks in various regions of the country confirming, ordaining, and preaching "with good Mr. Holly," translating his sermons into French. When Coxe departed for Jamaica on the second day of 1873, he left behind under Holly's unofficial direction a company of six priests and four deacons to carry on evangelical work in Haiti.[13]

Coxe's report, which was printed in the *Spirit of Missions,* the missionary magazine of the Episcopal Church, contained many half-truths, but Holly offered neither criticisms nor corrections. Indeed, one must suspect that in his eagerness to call Haiti to the attention of American churchmen he encouraged Coxe to paint a vivid picture. Coxe's article discussed the primitive religious conditions found in Haiti, complete with a description of either real or imagined barbarisms, superstitions, and incantations prevalent among the "poor natives" of the island. The important point was that Coxe's discussion of the horrors found in Haiti was counterbalanced by his glowing praise of the success Holly, "almost single-handed until now," had met with in Haiti.[14]

Holly had found in Coxe the ideal white churchman to push the mission in Haiti. A fellow bishop described Coxe as "vital, vivid . . . always in a fine frenzy over his work." Once back in the States, Coxe labored to secure increased appropriations for Haiti and the episcopate for Holly. He lectured widely about his trip, emphasizing that before the gospel could really take root Haiti had to have her own bishop.[15]

While Coxe promoted Holly's cause, Holly himself gradually assumed more and more administrative power. He found himself acting as de facto bishop in directing the work of the church. Under his leadership the annual convocation in 1871 had divided Haiti into distinct missionary districts. Holly frequently visited the outlying stations of the younger or less experienced workers. He also controlled all missionary mail going out to the United States. Thus he was able to mute effectively any news of dissension or internal criticism of his leadership.[16]

Less than six months after Bishop Coxe's visit Holly's expanding fortunes received a setback from a fire—political and incendiary in origin—that destroyed half the capital of Haiti. Consumed in the flames were Holy Trinity Church, the school, the rectory, the church printing press, and nearly all possessions of the Holly family. Holly was thankful that his family escaped unharmed, but was much grieved over the loss of his theological library collected over a period of twenty years. Within a week's time he had begun a new structure, "admittedly inferior," to house under one roof the church, the school, and the rectory. Funds for the building had been raised by the personal subscriptions of Ebenezer Bassett and other prominent residents of Port-au-Prince. Soon Holly opened a serious campaign to persuade the American church to build a stone church on a larger lot far removed from the government arsenal. Throughout the summer he supervised the construction of the new mission building, working fifteen hours a day, and bore the ever-increasing strain of feeding and housing his family in such difficult times. The burden proved too intense.[17]

On November 13, 1873, while at work soliciting church funds from merchants, Holly suffered a severe sunstroke and a sudden and massive contraction of the right side of his face. This was accompanied by a temporary paralysis of the tongue. For six weeks he lay critically ill. In January 1874 his condition bettered and he gradually regained his strength, although he was forbidden to leave his house until May. Temporarily chastened and convinced that "the decline of life is about setting in," Holly at age forty-five, repeated the theme of his first year in Haiti, of "dying the death of the righteous." But his spirits improved with the arrival of the long-hoped-for invitation from the foreign committee asking him to meet with the board of missions in the autumn in 1874 to discuss the question of a bishop for Haiti. Now revived, Holly renewed his correspondence with the foreign committee, Bishop Coxe, and other American churchmen. Within a period of three months the enthusiastic Holly sent seventy-two letters to the United States.[18]

## III

A "Special Committee on Haiti," chaired by Coxe and composed of bishops, clergy, and laity, had met in February 1874. It had passed a resolution that Haiti should have her own bishop, and had decided that James Theodore Holly should be called to the United States in the autumn of 1874 to consult with the foreign committee. It finally seemed possible for Holly to be elected bishop of Haiti. His only competition in Haiti for the position was his first recruit to the ministry, the Reverend St. Denis Bauduy. Though Bauduy was the favorite candidate of Bishop Alfred Lee, his age—he was seventy-one—precluded him from serious consideration.[19]

The special committee had briefly entertained the notion of sending a white man to head the Haitian mission in the same manner it had sent a white to direct church activities in Liberia. But this consideration died outright because the committee, led by Bishop Coxe, believed that under Haitian law only "a person of color" and a citizen could be the "superior ecclesiastic" of any religious body in Haiti. This was not true—the new constitution containing this stipulation had never been validated—but the committee remained ignorant of this fact and Holly did not hasten to set them right. Why should he? He knew himself to be both the best and the only suitable candidate for the bishopric of Haiti. In Coxe he had a powerful ally. The special committee followed Coxe's every suggestion because, as one member said, "the Bishop . . . speaks of things he has seen."[20]

Pursuant to the instructions of the foreign secretary, Holly presented himself in New York in early September 1874. Believing that he was on "display," he spoke to numerous missionary groups and women's auxiliary societies in New York and Washington. While in Washington he was presented by Howard University with the Doctor of Divinity degree he had long sought.[21]

Prior to the opening of the general convention of 1874 the "prospective candidate for the Bishopric of Haiti" met several times with a committee of five bishops. Among them were Coxe and the Anglican prelate of Jamaica, Bishop Reginald Courtenay, a friend of Holly. The question to be resolved was the future status of the church in Haiti: Should it be organized as a missionary district of the Protestant Episcopal church of the United States, or erected as an independent national church to be aided by the mother church in the United States? Holly, as dean of the Haitian convocation, had come to America "clothed with full powers" by that body to make a covenant with the Protestant Episcopal church of the United States to secure the recognition of the church in Haiti as an independent national church holding fraternal relations with the church in America.[22]

He gained everything he sought. A covenant drawn up between Holly and the House of Bishops recognized Haiti as a foreign church that was to receive during its infancy "missionary succor" from the American church. A permanent commission of four bishops, to include the first bishop of Haiti, was "to act in concert on all discipline belonging to that order . . . until there shall be three native Bishops in Haiti." The Haitian convocation, represented solely by Holly in these negotiations, pledged conformity to the "doctrines, worship and discipline" of the American church. On November 3, 1874, the House of Bishops formally elected James Theodore Holly to be the first bishop of Haiti.[23]

A large group of Negroes crowded into Grace Church in New York City on the evening of November 8, 1874, to witness Holly's consecration. Directing the ceremony was the presiding bishop of the American church, Benjamin Smith of Kentucky, who fifteen years before had issued a call for the consecration of Negroes to the episcopate. Among the other bishops laying on hands were Holly's steadfast supporters, Arthur Coxe and Reginald Courtenay. With his consecration Holly became the first Negro Episcopal bishop and the second black bishop of any major white Christian church in the world. Eleven days later Bishop Holly sailed for Haiti. While at sea he wrote Secretary Duane that "I feel my health sensibly invigorated by my visit and I now go to offer it as a new sacrifice to God."[24]

On his arrival in Port-au-Prince Holly found his parishioners and all the members of his family waiting to conduct him through a "hastily constructed triumphal arch" to Holy Trinity Church. There he preached his first sermon as bishop, saying of his rise to the episcopate that "human instruments and worldly power were of no value in this matter, but that the movements of God's Holy Spirit had been the basis of all our successes in the past." No matter what he preached, those close to the new bishop knew that the Holy Spirit had been amply helped out by the lobbying of James Theodore Holly.[25]

Three weeks after returning to the Black Republic Holly was solemnly invested by his own convocation as bishop of an independent Haitian church, the Orthodox Apostolic Church in Haiti. He subscribed to two oaths at the ceremony: to respect the canonical prerogatives of the national convocation, and to respect the national independence and sovereignty of the Haitian people by obeying the constitution, laws, and government of Haiti. In taking these pledges he found himself reaffirming the style of churchmanship he himself had composed and a principle he had eagerly followed since 1861.[36]

## IV

The months immediately following Holly's consecration were filled with what had been and was to remain a "usual" combination of routine duties and hardships. He conducted visitations to the outlying missionary districts and struggled to increase church membership during a time of political unrest and inflation. In February 1875 Port-au-Prince suffered through another fire. This time Holy Trinity Church was spared, but John P. Hepburn, Holly's former friend and more recent antagonist, was "burnt to death."[27]

Holly did make a brief trip to the United States in the autumn of 1875, his last such visit for the next twenty-one years, to place his two eldest sons in a Negro trade school in North Carolina. The struggling black institution gained in morale by having the children of Bishop Holly in attendance, but the journey further depleted Holly's finances.[28]

Foreign Secretary William Duane, Holly's effective, sympathetic, and influential friend at the Church Missions House, died suddenly in December 1875, leaving Holly with few allies on the foreign committee. Under these circumstances— which would persist in subsequent decades—he found himself turning for financial support, usually without much success, to other public and private sources in the United States and England.[29]

Missionaries, even if black and in Haiti, were obliged to eat. They also had to buy clothing, pay medical bills, educate their children, and do what other people normally did. James Theodore Holly never received enough salary to take care of his needs. Many of his fellow bishops in the United States or in foreign fields could depend on family money to supplement their salaries, but Holly enjoyed no inheritance and had ten children to educate. His financial situation, always plagued by indebtedness, was never more precarious than during the first decade of his episcopate, when he was virtually reduced to begging. At the risk of losing all pride, "for when self-respect is gone, manhood goes with it," he repeatedly asked church officials in the United States to bail him out of his difficulties. More often than not his answer came in the form of a box of used clothing donated by churchwomen's auxiliary groups.[30]

In 1877, because of the depressed economy in the United States and an accompanying drop in missionary operating funds, the Episcopal church drastically reduced expenditures in all foreign missionary fields. The normal appropriation to Haiti of $6,250, already meager in comparison to the funds allotted to other missions, was cut 25 percent for 1878, with a further reduction of 25 percent planned for 1879. The foreign committee justified this action by recalling that the Haitian mission had been undertaken by the board of missions in 1865 as "temporary and with the design to give partial and transient aid . . . to help the people of that island to enter upon an independent and permanent work." The reduction was a staggering blow to the struggling church in Haiti and a personal tragedy for the Holly family. The bishop's salary was to be cut from $1,800 to $1,350.[31]

News of the cut in salary reached Holly shortly after he had requested an increase to $2,400 for what he called "cogent reasons": children to feed, clothe, and educate, the "dear" cost of transportation in making his episcopal visitations around the island, and his personal indebtedness, much of it carried over from the days before he was bishop. Besides, he had recently used part of his salary to support a fledgling seminary in Port-au-Prince.[32]

When he got a reduction instead of an increase Holly criticized the foreign secretary, Joshua Kimber, for his ignorance of the high cost of living in Port-au-Prince, and asked if the American church was prepared to make eunuchs of its clergy by calling for celibacy. The only answers he received were further admonitions concerning his tendency to overdraw his account. The foreign committee also censured him for his audacity in requesting that money be taken from other church workers in Haiti to restore his old stipend of $1,800. Holly's argument was that the others all had secular jobs as government clerks or teachers, and the older missionaries such as Alexandre Battiste and Bauduy, whose families had grown up, could endure a reduction, whereas he could not. In rebuking Holly the foreign committee declined to raise his salary, but did adopt the reduced scale he had suggested for the other workers. In 1880 Holly's stipend was restored to $1,800 per annum. But the damage had been done. By then he was hopelessly in debt and hard pressed by creditors.[33]

In 1878 Holly enjoyed an opportunity to shake off for a time the specter of financial distress. The occasion was the Lambeth Conference in England where, during a visit of two months, he was able to bask in a succession of honors and to seek new sources of aid for his mission. The trip was made possible by the Haitian government. President Boisse Canal and his secretary of public worship, Dalbermarle Joseph, had noted the nationalistic aspirations of the Orthodox Apostolic Church in Haiti and its growing list of native clergy and lay converts. Canal in his annual presidential address of 1877 criticized the Roman church for a dearth of native priests and emphasized the "imperative" need for more Haitians to direct the religious life of the Republic. Joseph sympathized with Holly's hope that the Orthodox Apostolic Church would eventually become the church of all the people of Haiti. Holly was given $400 in gold to pay his travel expenses to Lambeth. There he was expected to secure from the Pan-Anglican Synod of Churches formal recognition for the church in Haiti and membership in the Anglican communion of churches.[34]

The foreign committee could not contribute any funds toward Holly's trip, but Acting Secretary Samuel Denison, who had been called out of retirement, was pleased as well as surprised to hear of it and wished the bishop "a good time in England." Even this felicitation was noteworthy, for relations between Holly and the foreign committee had been cool and letters infrequent since the reduction of the Haitian appropriation late in 1877.[35]

The conference that brought Holly to Lambeth was a gathering of thirty-six non-English bishops of the Anglican communion, either colonial or independent, and sixty-six English prelates to discuss "The Condition, Progress, and Needs of the Anglican Communion." The bishops formally met with the Archbishop of Canterbury at Lambeth Palace on July 2, 1878. Amidst the colorful robes and dazzling mitres of the professionals, the one black face was that of Bishop James Theodore Holly of Haiti. His complexion obviated for him any need to seek introductions or identify himself to his fellows. At Lambeth he shared, as one bishop wrote, "in the warmth of emotions . . . of a band of consecrated brothers, knit by the same link to the one Elder Brother in whose name we met."[36]

The Lambeth Conference of 1878 was only the second gathering of the Pan-Anglican Synod. The first conference ten years earlier had been the outcome of a search for increased unity among Anglican clerics throughout the world. This second meeting helped solidify the tradition of calling the Anglican community to meet every decade to discuss common questions of "unity, power, missionary work, ritualism, scepticism and disestablishment." Conferences were advisory, possessing no legislative or judicial power. Eventually conferences would attempt to deal with racial problems, but the conference of 1878 concerned itself strictly with ecclesiastical matters. The bishops attending deemed it "inexpedient" to publish an account of the debates.[37]

Of particular interest to the session of 1878 was the intention of the mother church in England to aid infant movements in independent states (most of them Roman Catholic) seeking "to reform their churches along the lines of the Church of England." Holly's Orthodox Apostolic Church in Haiti was the first autonomous national church established under Anglican auspices outside an English-speaking area. As such it marked the inauguration of a new policy and was recognized at Lambeth as a landmark accomplishment of the Anglican communion. Other autonomous churches of a nature similar to Holly's creation would subsequently be founded under Anglican auspices all over the world.[38]

Hospitality and friendship were lavished upon Holly during his six weeks in England. Except for a "severe" but brief recurrence of his nervous disorder of three years before, Holly's stay was "delightful." In London he found himself much in demand as a dinner guest. He met with the respect Negroes had long received from the British. None of the malignant racial hatred so prevalent in the United States had yet seeped into England. Holly was presented to Queen Victoria and dined with fellow bishops at a lavish feast sponsored by the Lord Mayor of London. On the evening of July 24, 1878, dinner companions at the home of Dean Arthur Stanley included three other distinguished Negroes, Edward Wilmot Blyden, Liberian diplomat and man of letters; King George of Bobby; and John M. Smyth, United States minister-resident in Liberia. Blyden wrote a friend that "For the first time, I believe, in the history of England have four persons of purely African descent so freely mingled with elite."[39]

Holly accepted Dean Stanley's invitation to become the first Negro to preach in the English shrine, Westminster Abbey. Both his selection and his eloquent sermon received much attention in England. The peroration was also printed in Negro newspapers in the United States and later reproduced in one of the first scholarly histories of the Negro in America:

And now on the shores of Old England, the Cradle of that Anglo-Saxon Christianity by which I have been in part, at least illuminated . . . I catch a fresh inspiration and new impulses of the divine missionary spirit of our common Christianity; and here in the presence of God, of angels and of men . . . I dedicate myself anew to the work of God, of the gospel of Christ and of the salvation of my fellow men in the far distant isle in the Caribbean that has become the chosen field of my special labors. . . .

Buoyed by his reception in England and by tentative promises of financial aid for both his church work and the education of his progeny, Holly returned to Haiti.[40]

# VIII     Troubles on Every Side

A photograph of James Theodore Holly reveals a man of slight build and erect stance with intense eyes. His actions show him tremendously energetic, impulsive, zealous, often self-righteous, and an eager participant in any controversy. He was so convinced of the wisdom of his beliefs that he was not simply dominating but downright domineering.

Despite his best efforts, the Orthodox Apostolic Church of Haiti seemed to lose ground during the decade after the Lambeth Conference. Much of this trouble could be attributed to decreased appropriations from the church in the United States, to the bishop's inability to control the ambitions of a few of his workers, and to an increased hostility among prominent American churchmen toward the independent status of the Haitian church.

## I

Disease and death, fire and revolution—these Holly could cope with; but the peril of being cut off from the financial aid of the American church, meager as it was, continued to be a major threat to his Orthodox Apostolic Church. When disaster struck in Haiti, churchmen in the United States were heard to grumble about "irresponsible Negroes" and their penchant for revolutions and destructive fires. New funds could usually be raised in America, however, to rebuild the physical structures. But any scandal touching the reputation of the bishop was another matter. If allowed to circulate unchallenged, even a rumor could destroy Holly and in turn bring down his church.

At the beginning of his missionary work in the Black Republic Holly had decided to cooperate with other Protestant groups in contesting the influence of the Roman Catholic church in Haiti. Thus when Holy Trinity Church was destroyed by fire on four separate occasions, he was able to conduct his services in the churches of either the Wesleyans or the African Methodist Episcopalians. But when rival denominations moved into areas where he had established missionary stations, there was often friction. Holly believed that the Wesleyans resented the gains made by his church. Periodically, these "left-handed brethren" would start a rumor designed to discredit him and the Orthodox Apostolic Church. In the spring of 1880, according to the bishop, the Wesleyans claimed that his recent visit to north Haiti had been politically motivated to spread division between pure Negroes and mulattoes. When little came of this charge, the Wesleyans then spread a story that Bishop Holly was preparing to renounce Protestantism and embrace Romanism. Holly squelched this rumor by asking how he was to find room in the Roman archbishop's seminary for his wife and six youngest children.[1]

Though Holly throughout his ministry in the Black Republic concentrated his main efforts and those of his coworkers on preaching to native Haitians, he felt at the same time an obligation to provide for the spiritual needs of the large number of English-speaking black immigrants from the neighboring West Indies. These people, ignorant of the French language and mostly unemployed, lived in a notorious slum, the Bel Air section of Port-au-Prince. Several times Holly opened an outdoor mission in Bel Air and employed one of his lay readers or young deacons to preach there. Then the pressure of expanded efforts in the countryside caused the Bel Air mission to be abandoned for months at a time. In 1874 Holly seemed to have an ideal candidate to minister permanently in Bel Air. He was the Reverend C. J. Bistoury, who had grown up in Bel Air. But Bistoury, after only a few months on the job, was killed by a bolt of lightning. Holly endeavored over the next ten years to find a suitable replacement, only to have a trio of men he assigned to Bel Air almost succeed in destroying his reputation.[2]

In 1879 the bishop appointed a recent immigrant to Haiti, the Reverend Andrew Perret, to assist another newcomer, the Reverend Joseph Durant, in the Bel Air mission. Perret, a native of France and a convert from Catholicism, had come to Haiti from the Diocese of New York. His arrival in September had been greeted with much fanfare by Holly. Within two months' time, however, Perret had to be removed from his post because of his "moral defects." Holly reported that "after some blustering" Perret retired from the field and rejoined the Romans.[3]

The bishop fared no better with Joseph Durant. A native of Maryland, Durant had been ordained to the diaconate in the Diocese of Pennsylvania. In 1876 he had been found guilty of "gross immorality" and ordered to leave Pennsylvania. Holly was aware of this background, but he needed an English-speaking clergyman for Bel Air. Convinced that Durant had "mended his character," Holly took him into the Haitian church. Soon Durant defied Holly's orders and influenced a lay reader and other members of the unruly Bel Air congregation to abandon the Orthodox Apostolic Church. When Holly deposed him in January 1881 Durant, unlike Perret, refused to drop out of sight. He vowed that he would write letters to influential churchmen in America to, as Holly put it, "bring me down." The implementation of Durant's threat set off a four-year period of charges and recriminations centering on the personal integrity of James Theodore Holly.[4]

Durant commissioned a friend in the neighboring Republic of Dominica to send slurs and incriminating allegations about Holly to a churchwoman in Boston. She then forwarded to the Church Missions House a series of protests that invoked the name and prestige of Major Robert Stuart, the British minister-resident in Port-au-Prince. The following quotation from this "unnamed" Bostonian, who had never met Holly or been to Haiti, illustrates how the seeds of doubt were first planted:

> If I were to write the truth of the way things go among the English Protestants in Haiti it would be unfit for publication. In Port-au-Prince, I am told, under Bishop Holly, the Episcopalians are making no progress at all; his reputation is anything but A 1. I have staying with me a month Major Stuart. He is perfectly disgusted with Bishop Holly's behavior and will have nothing to do with him; but because he has a nice little wife and ten children no one cares to deprive him of a living. Besides, morality is of no account in this country, and it would be hard to find someone to cast the first stone.[5]

The foreign secretary, Joshua Kimber, tried to suppress this attack on Holly's character. A "personal" letter to the bishop warned him of the rumors touching him. Holly promised that he would ask his "warm and devoted friend" Stuart to deny the accusation. But when Stuart, confronted by Holly, refused to do this, Kimber decided that an investigation was necessary. The secretary wrote directly to Major Stuart asking for written certification of the "unwarrantedness of the charges." Stuart answered that since his return to Haiti in February 1880 he had heard "for the first time" many stories about the bishop's private life, stories "quite at variance" with his previous opinion of Holly. He found that many residents of Port-au-Prince believed Holly had acted unwisely in removing Perret and Durant from the church. Although he offered no proof, the major ended his letter with a vague implication that the rumors about Holly might be true.[6]

These charges came at a time when Holly was already at odds with the foreign committee over his tendency to borrow on missionary funds. And more controversy involving another missionary in Bel Air, John Robert Love, soon added to the difficulties. Love was a complex Negro intellectual and a controversial pamphleteer. Born in Nassau, he became a lay reader in the Anglican church, emigrated to Florida where he was ordained a deacon in 1871, went as a curate to a church in Savannah, Georgia, and then moved to Buffalo, New York. There he studied medicine and was ordained a priest in 1877. At all three American locations Love's ambition combined with his physical attraction for married women in his congregation to earn him the displeasure of his diocesan bishop. In 1881, at the request of Bishop Arthur C. Coxe, Love moved to Haiti.[7]

Holly reluctantly deferred to the wishes of his friend Coxe and allowed Love to join the Haitian mission for a two-year probationary period. He was to support himself by practicing medicine while ministering to the people of Bel Air. In May 1881, shortly after Love's arrival, Holly praised his zeal "in healing both physical and spiritual wounds in Bel Air." A month later Love had gathered a "numerous congregation." By July the doctor's success stimulated Holly to begin laying plans for a permanent medical mission in Port-au-Prince.[8]

The warm feeling between the new recruit and his bishop ended abruptly when Love defied Holly's orders. A persuasive orator, Love had gained complete control of his English-speaking congregation in Bel Air. On his instructions they renounced their allegiance to Holly's church and pledged themselves to follow only Dr. Love. When Holly's move to heal this schism met a contemptuous rebuff, the bishop responded by temporarily suspending Love from the ministry. To conceal the difficulties from the foreign committee he submitted a vaguely worded report that Love had "resigned his pastoral charge," but would continue his medical practice.[9]

In Port-au-Prince the private charges and countercharges between Love and Holly became public after Love sent a statement "to a few prominent Churchmen in the United States." He accused Holly of fabricating his reports, desecrating the Lord's Day, ordaining ignorant men, encouraging adultery in his congregation, "fanning strife" with other denominations, purchasing land for himself with church funds, making improper advances to females, and expressing a desire to be elected to the senate of Haiti.[10]

In retaliation Bishop Holly issued a formal inhibition that ordered Love to cease forever "from the exercise of any ministerial functions as a priest of the Orthodox Apostolic Church." Love refused to comply. Instead he dared Holly to try and "speak a Priest *in* or *out* of the Church as you think fit," and demanded an ecclesiastical trial according to the constitution and canons of the Protestant Episcopal church of the United States. The foreign committee passed Love's charges on to the House of Bishops' overseeing committee on Haiti and Mexico, of which Alfred Lee was chairman. The committee, trying to head off a scandal, asked Holly to withdraw his inhibition on the ground that it was not in correct canonical form. At the same time the foreign committee seriously considered holding up "all special appropriations" for Haiti until the controversy had been solved.[11]

Holly's answer, written under pressure from Bishops Lee and Coxe, the two most influential members of the overseeing committee, was an "official" letter saying that "if necessary" he would allow "that miserable man to repent and to return to his first works all over again." But an accompanying "confidential" letter to Coxe elaborated on the motivation of Love's slanderous accusations. According to Holly, Love aimed to destroy the bishop's influence and reputation in the United States "in the hope that in some way I can be got rid of and he come to the Bishopric of Haiti." Holly added charges of his own. Love had refused to give communion to one of his parishioners, and he had "kept company" with a notorious prostitute, "saying that he was trying to reform her, convert her and marry her." When admonished by Holly, Love "flew into a passion" and acted with "outright disrespect." Love's "vindictive spirit" had led him "to out Herod, Herod, to surpass even Satan himself in his foul fabrications to injure me."[12]

After Love refused to acknowledge their requests for mediation, Bishops Coxe and Lee ordered Holly to appoint a committee to investigate Love's accusations. Holly named his two clerical associates, St. Denis Bauduy and Alexandre Battiste, and one layman, Alex Heraux, his personal attorney. On February 2, 1882, Battiste as chairman of the committee requested a series of interviews with Love, assuring him that only "a clear and impartial" statement of facts was sought. Love refused to be questioned. Four days later, Battiste, Bauduy, and Heraux reported to Bishop Lee:

> In regard to the charge of Profanation of the Sabbath we have heard some complaints . . . about the entrance of the milk-woman and the water carrier in the Bishop's house during the hours of divine worship. But in regards to the other charges, we have no knowledge of them whatsoever.[13]

When Love learned the contents of the report he wrote Lee that Holly should confess all the original charges, "which he can not even hope to disapprove." Holly had, he implied, "guided" the investigation by threatening to hold up the salaries of Battiste and Bauduy. Lee's committee refused to reply to Love's letter and urged Holly to bring him to trial despite his threat "to tell all to the American public."[14]

The trial to defrock Love was perfunctory at best. Holly was both judge and prosecutor; his son, Theodore Faustin, served as the clerk of the court; and the jury was composed of the bishop's loyal subordinates. The defendant was not even given adequate time in the courtroom to present his defense. When Love invited his former parishioners in Bel Air, men whom Holly called "disorderly low England subjects," to the trial, the bishop asked the secretary of state for public worship to keep these spectators away from the proceedings. The trial was conducted in English because Love spoke no French. Yet some members of the clerical jury did not understand English. On September 5, 1882, John Robert Love was deposed from the church for violations of the constitution and canons of the general convention and for breaking his ordination vows. No charge was pressed for immoral conduct.[15]

The formal deposition of Dr. Love from the church did not end Holly's problems with him. Love soon organized his own church and announced that three American bishops were coming to Haiti to consecrate him and put Holly on trial. He also wrote and published two pamphlets entitled *Is Bishop Holly Innocent?* and *Proof of Bishop Holly's Guilt.* These pamphlets, characterized by Holly as full of "lies, malice and misrepresentations," were widely circulated among Episcopalians in the United States.[16]

Love repeated the charge of immoral conduct, again without producing evidence. On the basis of Holly's reputation and career as a whole, it seems safe to discount and probably to dismiss these accusations. Love did make some valid albeit minor criticisms of Holly. It was true that Holly, when officiating, wore the scarlet hood of a university graduate, which he was not. Holly's vanity was no secret to Lee, Coxe, or the foreign secretary, but they knew that he believed he must impress the Haitians to compete with Roman Catholic ceremonials. They also recognized that occasionally his written reports made his exploits appear more noteworthy than they really were. This was, however, a common practice among missionaries eager to produce impressive statistics lest they suffer a reduction in support. Within days after Love's second pamphlet appeared in Port-au-Prince, one of Holly's loyal friends filed suit for slander against Love. On the eve of the trial Love volunteered as a physician in the government army and, in Holly's word, "abandoned his miserable attempt to collect a congregation and escaped the trial."[17]

Holly could now report that Love's career in Haiti, "a sham and a humbug," had ended; but the pamphlets had caused a stir in the United States. At the general convention in October 1883 Holly's conduct and his role in Love's deposition were discussed in veiled fashion on the floor of the House of Deputies. Secretary Kimber felt obliged to ask Holly to repeat the charges against Love because of the currency of a rumor "that the only charge of which he was found guilty was that of writing about yourself to the Haitian Commission of Bishops and the Foreign Committee." Holly at first refused on the grounds that he had dealt with Love "not only justly but mercifully" and that no more time should be wasted on "the most consummate rascal that I have ever met in my whole life." When it became obvious that the rumors were upsetting American contributors to the Haitian church, he relented and sent the foreign committee an account of the affair including a list of charges against Love. After considering the Love case and the state of the church in Haiti, the foreign committee directed Lee and Coxe to send a circular letter to church newspapers pointedly denying all of Love's accusations against Holly. The case was one of those "in which an unworthy minister, having been subjected to discipline seeks to revenge himself by attacking the character and course of his Bishop." Holly had won.[18]

In Holly's long career he experienced few problems with his native clergy, but literally every time he recruited from outside Haiti for priests he met with disaster. Soon after his troubles with Love another of his American workers embarrassed him. The Reverend Shadrack Kerr, on a trip to the United States to raise funds for a church in Cape Haitien, spent on himself all of the $1,200 he collected. He then fled to Jamaica, leaving behind several bad debts in Cape Haitien. News of this scandal appeared in the *New York Times*. Scarcely nine months later, in November 1884, another recruit, Julian Mercier of Jamaica, whom Holly had helped to educate, left his post in Bel Air and returned home to a higher paying job.[19]

Holly now refused to employ missionaries from either America or Jamaica. To Bishop Lee he wrote that even if some American churchmen were disposed to overlook because of the "disadvantages of race" the faults and ambitions of men such as Love, he would not. Holly continued to view the activity of Jamaican churchmen in Bel Air with a jaundiced eye. He felt "no sorrow" when many returned home. Here he was in rare agreement with the negrophobe and former British minister-resident in Haiti, Spenser St. John, who believed that "the natives of Haiti" were "infinitely superior to colonial negroes."[20]

## II

At the very time the Haitian church was threatened from within by Perret, Durant, and Love, a few American churchmen initiated a decade-long attack on its independent status. These men, led by Dr. Charles B. Hall, chairman during the 1870s of the foreign committee's study group on Latin American missions, believed that, if Holly's church was to be truly independent, all financial aid from the United States should cease.[21]

News of this threat to his church, and of a reduced appropriation for 1878–1879, stunned Holly. Only five months before, in June 1877, he had launched a plan to raise $50,000 in the United States and $100,000 in England to endow three permanent bishoprics in Haiti. Now he had to struggle simply to retain the regular yearly appropriation for the church. To Secretary Kimber he complained that self-supporting parishes should not be expected in a poor country such as Haiti after only sixteen years. At least a generation, or thirty years, would be required. The American church was violating her "nursing care" agreement and setting the Haitian church "adrift without even an endowment fund." Both Holly, burdened with debts, and the Haitian church, "mainly composed of poor people," would suffer greatly if the operating funds were cut off.[22]

By 1880 rumors were circulating in the United States that "nothing was being done" in Haiti. In June the foreign committee, unbeknown to Holly, suggested that "it would be better to put forth its efforts on a larger scale in Haiti or withdraw altogether from the field." The first proposal was not feasible in the depressed state of the committee's finances; the second was appealing. When the committee sought the opinions of Bishops Lee and Coxe, both men supported Holly, Coxe emphatically and Lee somewhat more hesitantly. Lee said that he would

> grieve to hear of the abandonment of the field by our church. Progress is no doubt slow . . . but it has been my hope that we are laying a good foundation . . . it is practically a heathen land. Bishop Holly seemed to have the qualifications for the work not easily found although not free from some drawbacks, such as a tendency to think more highly of himself than he ought to think. He would in my opinion be likely to effect more good in Haiti than in our Southern states.

Honoring the opinions of Coxe and Lee, the foreign committee continued to support the work in Haiti and even granted Holly's request of a year earlier for $1,800 with which to start a farm school.[23]

The question of the independent status of the Haitian church had not been resolved, however, and it was revived at the general convention in 1883. Hall, now retired from the foreign committee, addressed the House of Deputies. He was upset over the debt-ridden condition of the four-year-old Church of Jesus, a national Episcopal Church of Mexico led by Bishop Henry Riley, an Irish-American, and supported solely by the American church. The Church of Jesus had stubbornly refused to obey financial regulations of the foreign committee and had gone several thousand dollars in debt. In 1883, the committee of overseeing bishops for Haiti and Mexico broke the covenant with the Church of Jesus and requested and received Riley's resignation. But Riley's impetuous behavior in Mexico had jeopardized the future work of the church in Haiti. Hall wanted the American church to concentrate overseas work in Africa, Japan, and China, where she could convert true heathens rather than Christians of another denomination. Quite unjustly in the case of Haiti, he blamed the current indebtedness of the church's missionary program on the involvement in Mexico and Haiti. He saw nothing in the constitution of the American church authorizing it to assist in governing churches in Haiti and Mexico, and called for a "retreat" from both places.[24]

When accounts of Hall's speech reached Holly, he responded in several voluminous letters to Kimber and the foreign committee. Hall's "loose and inaccurate" statements demonstrated that the "good but naive brother" was confused. Considering that the American church had "for fifty years generously sustained the African Mission in an independent protestant republic composed of *English-*

speaking black Americans," then "why should Hall be in a hurry to ask for the end of a twenty-two year old mission established among a Roman Catholic French-speaking country?" Contrary to Hall's "side-winders," the bishop of Haiti was not an "irresponsible autocrat" nor should "the work in Haiti be put under a bushel because of its covenant." At a special meeting the foreign committee ordered Holly's letters printed and privately distributed among interested churchmen. His request that they be published in church newspapers was refused. Kimber explained to Holly: "You can not fail to see from the public prints how very sensitive the Church is just now upon the subject of Independent Churches. It is very uncomfortable for you but I do not see how it can be helped."[25]

The movement in the United States to seek a formal and final end to all missionary work in Haiti gradually subsided, although it flickered as late as 1887. In that year Hall published in the *Church Review* a long article that praised Holly but criticized the American church for helping the Orthodox Apostolic Church:

> It is proper to say that Bishop Holly has borne himself most worthily in his trying situation. . . . I pity him too, for we have kept him at starvation diet and shorn him to the quick. I frankly concede that if he could have brought up his difficult Mission to a true autonomy he would have done so; but I wish he were back again among his own race here at home; it would be better for us all.[26]

Holly answered in a series of letters to the *Advance*, a church newspaper in Baltimore. He denied that the Haitian church was "truly autonomous." A national church reached independence only when "able to perpetuate within itself the ancient historical Episcopate." To do this a church had to have three bishops, the number required to consecrate a new bishop. Thus, even though the Haitian church was staffed by natives and led by a naturalized citizen of the Republic, it still was not completely independent. Holly further suggested that each foreign mission field receive equal care from the mother church: "No invidious distinction should be made between them in the missionary policy of the Board of Missions." His poor church, he felt, should not be continually subjected to reduced budgets and harassed by threats of cutting off all aid. But it was.[27]

Holly's monetary problems continued to keep him in difficulty with the foreign committee. In rebuking him for his frequent overdrafts on the missionary treasury, Kimber remarked: "I had not understood when you said that you were running into debt to undertake your visitations, that you were running into debt to us!" The foreign committee ordered the treasurer to freeze the "Bishop's Contingent Fund" for special works in Haiti until Holly's salary account was balanced. Already Holly had written that he was once more being forced to turn to shoemaking to supplement his income. With no relief in sight from the United States, he related that he had to "trust to Providence to find some way to tide me over my embarrassments." Aid finally came in the form of a personal loan from a wealthy friend in Haiti who believed that the bishop had better ways to spend his time than making shoes.[28]

# IX

# Defender of the Race

"I am a Negro," wrote James Theodore Holly; "I love my race; I am not ashamed of my identity with them. I declare this in season and out of season." He was, as one of his sons recorded, "a race man in every possible sense. . . . His faith in the ultimate redemption and elevation of Africa and her children . . . was of the kind which made God pleased." Holly never hesitated to speak out against any individual or institution, black or white, that offended, in his view, him, Haiti, or the African race. Sometimes to the embarrassment of his friends, his voice thundered in denunciation of unrestrained capitalism and imperialism both in Haiti and elsewhere; but, as he declared early in his career, he must "follow a sense of duty."[1]

## I

Sir Spenser St. John, who served as British minister-resident and consul general in Haiti from 1863 until 1875, described himself as the "intimate" friend of both Ebenezer Bassett and James Theodore Holly. He lived next door to Bassett, attended Holly's church, and endorsed requests for contributions that Holly mailed to England. In 1883, eight years after he had left the country, St. John published *Hayti; or the Black Republic*. In the introduction he pledged himself to be both "above racial prejudice" and a friend to Haitians "of all ranks and shades of color." Yet, because "it is necessary to describe a people as they are, and not as one would wish them to be," criticism was offered.[2]

The prevailing theme of St. John's book may be gathered from a single passage:

> I now agree with those who deny that the negro could ever originate a civilization, and that with the best of educations he remains an inferior type of man. He has shown himself totally unfit for self-government and incapable as a people to make any progress whatever. To judge the negroes fairly, one must live a considerable time in their midst and not be led away by the theory that all races are capable of equal advance in civilization.

According to St. John, Haitian society was coarse and brutal. Gradual elimination of the mulatto element produced a condition of unadulterated negroism—"the awkward figure, heavy face, the bullet head, the uncouth figure, the cunning blood-shot eyes." Haitian history was nothing but a series of plots, revolutions, and bar-baric military executions. The capital city was "the filthiest town" St. John had ever seen, the island republic was "the country to be avoided," and the Negro race was "hopeless." The crowning Haitian sin was the superstitious African fetish-ism of Vodun (Voodoo) and its accompanying cannibalism.

St. John was relatively kind in his published description of Holly. Though point-edly called a "black," Holly received praise for possessing "many of the qualities which ensure a good reception . . . pleasant manners, well educated, and . . . thor-oughly in earnest." In other words, he was not a typical Haitian.[3]

St. John's book provoked Holly and two of his sons, Theodore Faustin and Alonzo Potter Burgess, into quick defense of their homeland. Their response followed two patterns: veiled insinuations that St. John's behavior in Haiti had been scan-dalous, and attempts to explain the "extenuating circumstances" for many of Haiti's admitted problems.[4]

In letters to T. Thomas Fortune, editor of the New York *Freeman*, Bishop Holly sought to dismiss "the silly book of the trifler Spenser St. John." The author was little more than a "foreign adventurer." When asked by Foreign Secretary Joshua Kimber about the book, Holly answered by alluding to St. John's "personal record known to all men acquainted with him. The most I will say is that he who lived in a glass house should not throw stones." Frederick Douglass, who had been Amer-ican minister-resident to Haiti, later spoke of St. John as "a man who left Haiti with a reputation which no honest or pure man can desire for himself."[5]

Holly—who feared that the "simple-minded public in Great Britain" would be-lieve St. John and lose interest in sending missionary funds to Haiti—informed the English press that St. John's book, though valid on many points, presented an unfair and grossly distorted picture of Haiti. People had to remember, he argued, that the country had been brutalized by generations of slavery and oppression, deserted by missionaries, and corrupted by the examples of foreigners of wealth and position "who without the same excuse, indulged in the same profligacy as the natives."[6]

To Negroes in the United States Holly's two sons explained that Haiti, a "young nation," was going through a rapid evolution. Alonzo observed that "we have been criticized for our revolutions which certainly are abuses in themselves but which undoubtedly have historical precedents." Readers of the New York *Free-man* had to be aware, he went on, that "at the time the race [in America] was grovelling in ignominy, Haiti first gave proof of the abilities of the Negro race." Both Alonzo and Theodore Faustin Holly criticized St. John's discussion of canni-balism. Speaking at a Brooklyn literary meeting, Alonzo acknowledged one "authenticated case" in 1863 that had brought severe punishment to its perpetrators. Theodore dismissed claims of man-eating as "antiquated hearsay."[7]

Despite the efforts of the three Hollys and other defenders, the image of Voodoo, cannibalism, illiteracy, and brutality in Haiti so vividly established by St. John persisted. Indeed, his book would remain the standard interpretive work on Haiti until well into the twentieth century.[8]

## II

Throughout Holly's residence Haiti was periodically wracked by revolution, "the chronic state of Haitian society." In his letters to church leaders in the United States he alternately fulminated against and defended this characteristic of his adopted country, but he never gave up hope that stability would be achieved. On the favorable side, he saw the revolutions as "helping the cause of the gospel." He believed that in times of trouble people in Haiti, like their brethren elsewhere in the world, either joined or returned to church.[9]

Holly was never consistent in his opinions about Haitian politics. Early in his missionary career, when the ravages of fire touched him and his workers, he bemoaned the general state of lawlessness. "No other race but the Saxon race seems to understand political constitutions." More commonly he defended Haiti's political behavior, though the defense might sound somewhat specious. For example, he once retorted to Haiti's critics in the United States that her "stirring revolutions in which one government was upturned to install another to be soon upturned in the same way" were equivalent to an "election spree" in the United States. In 1876 he wrote Secretary Denison that "not as many lives are lost in Haiti as at one of your ward precincts in a New York election day." When Haiti in 1888 experienced its sixth rebellion since his arrival in 1861, Holly maintained that the period after revolutions illustrated "to a most remarkable degree" that Haiti had the "secret of self-government." She was able to preserve public order and tranquility between the time the official government fell and the new administration took office.[10]

Only two presidents of Haiti in Holly's time were mulattoes. The power of an army controlled by black generals, and the distrust of the black masses were almost too much for a mulatto president. But the light-skinned elite was able to manipulate insurrections to maneuver its favorite black general into power, and then to assume the various ministerial and other offices. This pattern of behavior, "the greatest hindrance to Haiti's evolution," disgusted Holly, who had little use for the mulattoes. He called them an "unpatriotic class of Haitians who would fain [think] themselves the cream of society" and who "never had one grain of sympathy for the toiling masses who compose the majority of their fellow countrymen." He preached against conspiracy and rebellion, "the blackest crimes of Satan," and demanded a "reverence for law and order."[11]

Holly professed amazement that the so-called "better sort," many of whose pretensions were based on their "bastardy," were not as well behaved as the hardworking lower classes of the cities and the rural population. The poor of the countryside, "in their blissful ignorance are yet uncontaminated." Unlike Alexander Crummell and Edward Wilmot Blyden, his race-conscious friends in Liberia, Holly shied away from any color-caste political movement. He did agree with these men, however, that in Haiti, as in Liberia, the ultimate hope for the race lay with the "genuine" Negro. Holly was accused of fomenting racial trouble against the mulattoes, but there is no proof that he was ever active in a movement to rid Haiti of her impure strains.[12]

In spite of his disgust with Haiti's tendency to lurch from one government to another, Bishop Holly always differentiated very carefully between outright insurrections primed by "foreign adventurers of the rascally big nations" and a "supreme referendum" by the citizens of Haiti. In discussing the "impudent" attempt of retiring President Simon Sam in 1902 to name his own successor by bribing the legislative assemblies, Holly explained how a "supreme referendum" worked. "The people chased off the delegates and locked up the chamber." It was "a wonderful piece of political surgery."[13]

Holly distrusted legislators, even though many were his friends. He saw little difference between their "talking and skylarking" and the activities of legislative bodies in other western countries; all were about as useful as "the fifth wheel on a coach." He was even less charitable in his opinion of appointed bureaucrats, "men who assume the facility of suspending or executing the laws as the notion takes them."[14]

When asked to list the most serious problems facing Haiti, Holly replied that the island was the "Mary Magdalene of nations," possessed of seven devils: her own mulatto sons, the Roman clergy, "extra-officious" diplomats and consuls from abroad, foreign adventurers and unprincipled speculators, African fetishism, the unjust impositions of outside powers, and the "gross ignorance of her masses." Yet he did not despair of progress. Had not Haiti maintained her own government since 1804? He often reminded the Republic's critics, black and white, of the lynch law in the American South and the violence surrounding striking workers in the North.[15]

Holly was ever a defender, constructive critic, and faithful lover of his black, or Hametic, brethren, be they in Haiti, Africa, or the United States. In 1889 Bishop Alfred Randolph of Virginia delineated to a white audience the manner in which the Negro differed from the white man. "Place him in a position where he is called to exercise his faculties . . . he is bewildered, he loses his head, he is inaccessible to ideas . . . he is without fixed purpose, steadiness of aim, and self-control." The white clergy of Virginia, agreeing with their bishop, voted to exclude black churchmen from membership in the diocese. When eight Negroes publicly protested this action, Holly applauded their spirit. He denounced the current white leadership of the church in Virginia, though not, of course, the Episcopal faith. The clergy he saw as only a temporary hindrance—the faith was still indispensable to the Negro. Long after the misguided white Episcopalians of Virginia were dead the Anglican communion in its "purity of spiritual order and liturgical services" would continue to be the "saving word of inspiration to the African race."[16]

So convinced was Holly of his own wisdom and vision that he dispensed unsolicited political advice to American Negroes. He was not above lecturing even as experienced a campaigner as Frederick Douglass. The bishop of Haiti felt nothing but contempt for American Negroes who persisted in voting Republican in every election. By the mid-1880s he believed that the party of Lincoln had abandoned and betrayed the Negro to "subserve" [the Republican Party's] personal interests." Acknowledging that "political scoundrels abounded in both parties," he once admonished Douglass to support the best man "regardless of what may be his party affiliation." Increasingly Holly came to favor Grover Cleveland, somehow overlooking the prejudices of Cleveland and the Democratic Party.[17]

Holly based much of his displeasure with Republicans and zeal for Democrats on the diplomatic stance of the two parties toward Haiti. Time after time he returned to this one criterion by which he gauged his opinions. The bishop always assumed that American diplomats sent to Haiti could serve most honorably by looking out for the interests of the Haitian people as well as those of the United States. His friend Ebenezer Bassett had done well by Holly's definition, and he was delighted when another Negro friend (or at least acquaintance), John Mercer Langston, succeeded Bassett as minister-resident in 1877. Holly met Langston on his arrival in Port-au-Prince prepared to be of service until Langston could become familiar with Haitian customs and the French language. Actually, Langston appears not to have sought such assistance, but initially Holly was nonetheless pleased with him and with his statement that the people of Haiti were "owners of a great country, the founders and builders of a great government and a national sovereignty and power respected and honored by all . . . the civilized powers of the world." In an account of Langston's first months in Haiti written for American publication Holly praised the minister's "open and frank deportment" and pronounced him a "worthy and high-toned" helper for the people of Haiti.[18]

The relationship cooled when the minister-resident engineered what Holly termed "outrageous" demands on the government of Haiti. First Langston pressed a highly dubious suit in favor of Adrian Lazare, a speculator who served as his personal secretary. Then he backed a claim by Antonio Pelletier, an American citizen who had been found guilty of slave trading in 1861. Pelletier escaped from jail and sued the Haitian government for punitive damages. Holly in a letter to the New York *Age* condemned the "pirate Pelletier" and his "pettifogging advocate," Langston, who must "answer to the Negro race for whatever responsibility he may have in this dirty business." Holly's argument moved Editor E. A. Fortune of the *Age* to run an editorial, "Robbing Hayti," which echoed Holly in demanding to know, in the name of the "colored people of the U.S.," why Langston supported the claim.[19]

Holly's other major grievance against Langston arose over a suit filed by one of Holly's fellow missionaries in Haiti, the Reverend C. M. Mossell, who represented the African Methodist Episcopal Church. According to Langston's report, Mossell, his wife, and daughter had suffered greatly during the revolution of 1884. Even though an article in the constitution of 1879 stipulated that "no Haytian or foreigner can claim damage for losses during civil trouble," Langston pressed a suit for $10,000 to compensate for destruction of property but also for "insults and abuses" inflicted upon the Mossells. This "swindle" so angered the bishop that he accused Mossell of "selling the cause of his master for 333 times as many pieces of gold as Judas obtained for his treachery," and then abandoning his congregation in Haiti to enjoy his "ill-gotten gains at home." Holly's charges provoked the New York *Age* to adjudge that Mossell's claims "possess very few elements of equity" and to call for an investigation by the A. M. E. general convention. The bishop was effectively answered, however, by H. C. C. Astwood, the black United States consul to the Republic of Dominica. Astwood wrote the *Age* to correct the "false impressions" and the "great injustices" done Langston by Holly, whom he called "an able man, strong on polemics but subtle and dangerous as an enemy." Pointing out that an American minister to Haiti was sent there to represent the United States, not to sympathize with the Haitian people, Astwood praised Langston and his handling of the Mossell case. As for Holly, he "would do more good for his people if he would employ his time and talent educating them to the fact that outrage, fire and sword are not the best means ... to vent political anger." For once Holly did not make a public rebuttal, although in his private correspondence he continued to castigate Langston and Mossell.[20]

Between July 1889 and July 1891 Frederick Douglass was America's minister-resident in Haiti. He and Holly differed in antebellum days, but as a diplomat Holly gave him high marks. Douglass found himself involved in a diplomatic maneuver to secure the Haitian port of Mole St. Nicholas for a coaling station for the American Navy. Aware of the strong nationalistic feeling in Haiti, Douglass realized that the government of Florvil Hyppolite would fall if it disposed of the Mole. Holly had been kept abreast of the negotiations through his relationship with principals in the Haitian government and the American delegation. He was a personal friend of President Hyppolite, and two of his sons served on the presidential staff. His friend, Ebenezer Bassett, had returned to Haiti as Douglass's personal secretary. And another of Holly's coworkers in Port-au-Prince, Alexandre Battiste, was a deputy consul for the American legation. In January 1891 five American warships anchored in the harbor of Port-au-Prince. This first American attempt ever at "gunboat diplomacy" in Haiti hastened Douglass's return home in May 1891. The Mole affair, which has been called "one of the most unsavory episodes in the history of American diplomacy," brought Holly to Douglass's defense. He translated all of Douglass's reports concerning the Mole for the French language newspapers in the capital and remained proud of Douglass's aupport of Haiti and "our race."[21]

## III

Concerning the major world problems of the late nineteenth century, James Theodore Holly often entertained decided opinions and was quite likely to offer ready answers based upon the "latest truths found in the Scriptures." He felt, understandably enough, a marked antipathy to world imperialism. Fond of describing Satan as the "first imperialist," he wryly noted that the "so-called great nations" had outshone their predecessor in this sphere. Holly defined imperialism as "the law of hell for the arbitrary annexation of other people's territory by a more powerful force of men." The reason "small tribes and nations" such as Haiti had long been involved in "civil commotions of parties, sections and cliques," was that large and powerful nations such as the United States and England avoided "intestine commotions by engaging instead in foreign wars to assert their dominance over weaker peoples." They also established colonies to draw away from their land the most "adventurous turbulent rascals who otherwise would disturb the home peace."[22]

In this social philosophy Holly could be judged a "radical" by the standards of most Negroes living in the United States at the turn of the century. Although he trusted in God to offer the remedy, Holly eagerly endorsed any movement that promised social and political relief for laboring men and women of any race anywhere in the world. Thus he applauded the brief surge of the Colored Farmers Alliance in the Southern United States as "a gathering political and social cyclone about to sweep through America and the world . . . as the deliberate reaction of the masses against the financial imperialism of the few."[23]

It was obvious to Holly that the working classes, producers of the world's wealth, were viciously exploited by the rich. His favorite illustration was Andrew

Carnegie and the suppression of the Homestead Steel strike in 1892. "Exploiters" also monopolized the land, which by right belonged to all the people. Each family was entitled to a homestead and a means of gaining a livelihood by "honest labor." He denounced the capitalistic rapacity practiced against the masses in every nation by "unprincipled land monopolists aided by political administrations." Greed existed because modern industry was without morality.[24]

Opinions of this sort, most of them presented between 1880 and 1900 in the pages of a "race" magazine, the *African Methodist Episcopal Review,* mark Holly as one of the first Negro intellectuals to expound the rudiments of a thesis of class conflict and to identify the mutual interests of white and black workers.

Although not a practicing economist, Holly considered himself well versed in the "dismal science." As a bimetallist in the 1890s he believed that advocates of a single gold standard were part of a great world conspiracy against the well-being of the laboring class. "Conspiring Shylocks" in the United States government and other financial centers of the world were "annihilating" the international trade value of silver as a money standard, thereby strengthening their control over the price of labor and the products of domestic industry in every country, and reducing wages to the lowest possible level.[25]

The list of economic reforms that Holly demanded of governments was comprehensive. Laws should regulate the size of companies, set standards for minimum wages and hours, and enforce revenue sharing on all profits over 6 percent, he believed. He also felt governments should require adequate housing for all people, preferably with the state as landlord. Unfair taxation, protective tariffs, and "vast military expenditures" had to stop. Only through these reforms could the world enter the twentieth century in a truly Christian manner.[26]

Holly's solutions were meant to be temporary. The "isms of cracked-brained enthusiasts"—nihilism, socialism, communism—were not the final answer. Only the second coming of Jesus Christ could save the masses from their oppressors. Holly based his belief in the millennium on a literal interpretation of the Bible, "the rule of my faith." Trust in God's ultimate judgment was not new to Holly. Variations of the same message appear in his published and private writings over a period of fifty years. He spoke of the coming "Kingdom of Christ" as early as 1860, and in later years became more obsessed with this prediction. "I must hurry my work before the end of the gospel dispensation shuts down upon the world (Matthew 24:14) and the terrible judgments now everywhere preparing to be let loose upon the earth (Isaiah 26:9)."[27]

From his study of the Scriptures Holly believed that the day of reckoning would occur sometime between 1876 and 1916. In 1876, according to his calculations, six-thousand years of human labor and sorrow had passed since the six days of God's Creation. A period of great tribulation would follow this time and then, according to the Seventy-second Psalm, the Prince of Peace "shall save the children of the needy and He shall break in pieces the oppressor." Only then could the destiny of men "religiously, politically, and economically" come to pass. Holly's reading of the Bible had convinced him that the "time of tribulation" would be forty years. Therefore, he arrived at 1916 as the end of the gospel dispensation. In that year or at some time during the preceding forty "all the iniquitous imperialism of the earth shall be turned into hell together with all the nations that forgot God." Writing in 1902 to the associate secretary, Joshua Kimber, on the possibility of a world war, Holly warned that the years were fast approaching when "all the blood-thirsty nations of the world would be smashed up in the apocalyptic destruction."[28]

Three years earlier, in 1899, Holly had been asked by the editor of the *Arena,* a periodical self-described as "liberal in religion, radical in politics and vehement in its oppositions to social wrongs," to contribute to a symposium entitled "The Race Problem." The only non-American and the only clerical participant, Holly found himself in the company of Negro journalists and educators, including Booker T. Washington. Although the editor was bemused by the unorthodox contents of Holly's article on "The Origin of Race Antagonism," it was printed beside the more conventional arguments of the other contributors. Holly defined the enemy of both God and man as imperialism, "a triple-headed Cerberus which has a political and financial head as well as a clerical one." The "so-called Christian and civilized nations" he denounced as "hordes of savages glorying in the wholesale assassinations of human beings by armies and navies . . . and absolutely incapable of solving the problem of the antagonism of races." He branded as a fool anyone who believed that the United States, "run by politicians of the worst sort . . . tools of great soulless financial corporations . . . can solve this problem of races gathered under the American banner except in the stronger brute-force of wholesale assassination." Clerical imperialism "through its manifold divisions and sectarian rivalry" had brought no answers. The only possible solution must come "through the shock of the most awful social cataclysm that has ever taken place on earth." At that time every nation and all people would be placed under the direction of "the Lord and His Christ."[29]

One must reemphasize that Holly's belief in the coming of the millennium and the deliverance of the Negro race was of long standing. He had affirmed it during his sermon at Westminster Abbey in 1878. There he preached that his race, after thousands of years in servitude, had possessed a claim on God's mercy since the time of Christ's crucifixion. On that day, Simon of Cyrene, of the Hametic or Negro race, helped Jesus carry his cross. Thus, said Holly, when "God comes" to earth the Hametic race will not be forgotten. Only then will the black man be truly free.[30]

# X

# The Bishop of Haiti

Holly believed that God had meant for him, through the Orthodox Apostolic Church of Haiti, to convey a constant message of encouragement and hope to his people. While he grew old in the service of his church, his adopted land continued to suffer devastation and turmoil. In the later decades of his life, however, he tended to discount (although he could never ignore) these troubles and to rest his hopes on a moral uplifting of the Haitian people through religion and education.

## I

So convinced was Holly that his church would become the church of all Haitians that he even attempted to attract the mulattoes, of whom he disapproved as a class, into the church. An experienced Masonic leader and scholar, he visited the Masonic temples in Haiti to win friends among their elitist members. He was willing, as the violently anti-Masonic Roman clergy were not, to conduct Masonic burial services. He delighted in reminding the mulattoes that only three public organizations in Haiti had autonomous native administrations: the government, the Masonic fraternity, and the Orthodox Apostolic Church. For their part, the mulattoes tolerated Holly's church, but he made few converts among them.[1]

The greatest opportunity to advance the church lay among the peasantry. Holly accordingly encouraged his clergy to put its best effort into reaching "the great mass who are practically heathen." But to do this he needed to supplement the incomes of his workers, many of whom labored during the week in secular jobs, usually teaching or farming, and could, therefore, devote only their evening hours and Sundays to the propagation of the faith. Time after time the bishop pleaded with church officials, and time after time he received the same reply: Why could not the Haitians support their own parish priests? What these critics did not take into account was the effort required of the Haitian peasant simply to provide labor and small sums of money to build modest chapels. Episcopal missions in other fields received from the United States funds adequate for salaries and for the erection of mission buildings. Yet Holly had to badger the board of managers of the Domestic and Foreign Missionary Society merely to maintain the status quo.[2]

Only a bishop could confirm new members into the Episcopal Church and ordain candidates for holy orders. Holly therefore undertook extensive journeys around Haiti to mission stations. For several years, however, he did not receive the discretionary or travel allowance that the American church granted its missionary bishops. To make episcopal visits, which could last as long as six weeks, he was frequently forced to borrow in advance against his salary. This kind of overdraft did not endear him to the treasurer of the board of missions.[3]

Holly's missionary trips were strenuous. To visit Pierre Jones at Jacmel, for example, he had to cross eighty-odd streams along the way. Even a short journey into the mountains outside Port-au-Prince meant a twelve-hour ride on a rented horse. Because he was not a good equestrian, these expeditions were especially hazardous for Holly, and he often ended up "quite battered." He once explained to the foreign secretary that he was forced to write while lying flat on his stomach because he was "suffering from a large abscess caused by a rough saddle and a hard-trotting horse." In his eightieth year the bishop still undertook his visits. His only concession to age was the replacement of the horse by a slower, "surer footed" mule.[4]

Holly and his clergy were not always welcomed with enthusiasm by their potential converts in rural Haiti. Accustomed to white Roman priests, many of the peasants could not accept a black man as a proper teacher of the Christian faith. They expected a black to lead the rites of the Vodun. Even in the immediate area around the capital Holly's missionaries occasionally met resistance. Especially when the country was in the midst of a revolution was there peasant opposition to all Protestants—clergy and laity alike. Men coming out of a Protestant church service might be seized, put into prison, or conscripted into the army. The French priests exacerbated hostile feelings by telling the people that all Protestants were traitors to their country. Although most harassment of this sort occurred during Holly's first decades in Haiti, his workers experienced occasional opposition as late as the early 1900s.[5]

The priests and deacons of the Orthodox Apostolic Church of Haiti had to teach the gospel to people who could not read the Bible or understand the French translation of the Prayer Book liturgy. In addition, the sharp, uncompromising stance of Holly's church toward the folk religion of Vodun hindered its ability to win genuine converts. The number of baptisms recorded by the bishop and his workers are misleading, for baptism was similar to a Vodun ritual, and many children were baptized in the name of Christ whose parents had no intention of raising them as Christian. The number of active communicants contrasted sharply with the number of baptized, but nonpracticing members. In 1874, there were only 250 communicants in the church, yet Holly and his clergy had baptized over five times that number of children. As long as priests baptized children of nonmembers, the baptismal record was high but meaningless.[6]

Despite the scarcity of confirmed communicants the clergy of the Orthodox Apostolic Church did make a mark in education. Small schools in the interior of the country opened up by Holly, his clergy, and lay readers served a real need. Because the Haitian government did not set great value on education, most of its citizens were illiterate. Holly and his church, which was active in three of the five government districts, established some basic goals regarding education: "To render the rising generation under our hands capable of reading the Bible and Book of Common Prayer. To make them useful to themselves in the ordinary business of life we teach them writing and the fundamental rules of arithmetic." This was the practical aim of the church's education work. In 1911, fifty-four small schools were operating under Holly's supervision.[7]

Although the New Haven colony's agricultural settlement on the Drouillard plantation had failed in 1862, Holly never completely abandoned the idea of teaching his black countrymen improved agricultural methods and "Christian civilization." He believed that "if society is to be saved, intelligent men must now turn their attention to developing the agricultural resources of the country." After becoming bishop he wanted to open a "Normal School and Collegiate Institution" near Port-au-Prince, a school which he visualized as a future "University of the Antilles." He dreamed of an appropriation of $5,000 annually from the American church to be used for fifty scholarships of $100 each to train agricultural teachers, who would open their own schools in the interior. After several years of seeking funds the bishop received in 1880 the sum of $1,800, which enabled him to buy fifty-seven acres outside the capital for a mechanical and farm school. He then sought money for buildings, farm implements, a portable sawmill, and a horse and wagon. But the enterprise was paralyzed from the start. Expecting to plant cotton as early as 1881, Holly was still trying in 1904 to find an honest overseer who knew how to cultivate this crop. Even when the proposed number of students was reduced to five a year, the bishop still could not find adequate support for the operation . He himself spent many days at the farm site, but he was never a skilled farmer. He could, and did, help harvest, but he could not make plants grow. By 1885 only one student remained at the farm school. During the next fifteen years the school served as little more than a residence for the bishop, who had been burned out of his rectory in 1888. At the turn of the century he once more sought financing to reopen the school, to be directed by his son Robert, but the outcome was the familiar one: no money to secure provisions, implements, or instructors.[8]

Another of Holly's persistent hopes in education was that of establishing a seminary in Port-au-Prince to train natives for the priesthood. He had planned in 1872 to use the two Haitians who had studied in the United States, Charles E. Benedict and Pierre E. Jones, to serve along with himself as professors in such a seminary. The foreign committee vetoed the idea, however, and assigned Jones and Benedict to missions far removed from the capital. Holly did not give up. He believed that theological training for Haitians should be offered in Haiti. Candidates who went abroad to study might refuse to come home, or, if they did return, might leave the mission and find better paying jobs. Impelled by these considerations the bishop managed to operate a seminary in Port-au-Prince for short periods of time, terminated usually by fire, revolution, or shortage of funds. Finally in 1901 Pierre Jones came to the capital to be dean of a new seminary, and this one proved so successful that a second opened four years later in Aux Cayes.[9]

A third area of the bishop's master plan to "uplift" Haiti centered around the healing of the sick—"an indispensable part of true gospel work." Holly had always kept medicines and treated the sick and poor in his parish. But his individual and often crude treatment was futile in combating the frequent epidemics of smallpox, yellow fever, typhoid, and influenza. The mission needed trained doctors to staff a permanent, well-equipped clinic or hospital in Port-au-Prince. Remembering the troubles caused by his first missionary physician, John Robert Love, Holly decided in 1885 to place all medical work under the supervision of his son, Dr. Alonzo Potter Burgess Holly. But the board of managers refused the bishop's request for $12,000 with which to establish a clinic and chapel in Bel Air, and they also denied Alonzo's appointment to the mission staff. A similar appeal to the American Church Missionary Society went unheeded. In 1895 Bishop Holly resubmitted his plans for a permanent medical station, which the board of managers deemed "inopportune." Six years later Holly and another son, Dr. Arthur C. Holly, borrowed money to open a temporary clinic. But his dream of a permanent, soundly endowed hospital was never realized. The project was finally abandoned in 1915 when the United States Marines occupied Port-au-Prince.[10]

One of Holly's largest accomplishments in the 1890s was not a new project but the completion of an old one. On July 4, 1888, Holy Trinity Church, the parsonage, and all of Holly's personal papers and belongings had been destroyed by fire. Writing to the general secretary, William Langford, the bishop remarked that "I am cast down but by no means discouraged." He soon had good reason to be, for the replacement of the church proved to be a seven-year project. After two years of negotiations Holly secured from the Haitian government a new lot several blocks distant from the government arsenal. Few Americans, however, responded to Holly's appeal for funds, and the cornerstone for the church was not laid until 1891. After waiting another twenty-four months in vain for contributions, the bishop took what he raised in Haiti, about $3,000, borrowed approximately as much again, and proceeded to direct the construction of a brick-and-iron church. By borrowing, Holly was, as he realized, courting financial disaster for himself and his church at a time of international financial uncertainty. And he had been warned by Secretary Langford that "because of the unstable condition of political affairs on the island of Haiti, our people of charitable impulse do not feel willing to contribute in that direction." Finally, with Holly's creditors demanding repayment, William Low of Brooklyn, a member of the board of managers of the Domestic and Foreign Missionary Society, paid off the balance on the note. Low also settled the debt Holly had incurred because of his medical clinic.[11]

Holly had declined an "expenses-paid" trip to America in 1895 because he was involved in "finishing up the new church." He and his daughter, Grace Theodora, were able to get away the following year, however, on the bishop's first visit to America in twenty-one years. Although he would stay in the United States less than a month, Holly busied himself in promoting the cause of the Haitian church. He delivered missionary addresses and preached in many locations, traveling as far west as Cincinnati. While in New York City he wrote a booklet intended to explain Haiti's "spiritual claim on loyal churchmen . . . and make known the crying needs of our missionary work." But neither his talks nor the booklet produced any contributors. Holly had predicted before visiting the United States that the "hub bub of the U.S. presidential election will crowd out of men's minds the proper consideration of Eternal Things." Now it was clear that his prediction had been correct.[12]

## II

One of Holly's major contributions to Haiti was his own procreation. Ten of fifteen children born to him between 1853 and 1878 survived into adulthood. Subscribing to the dictum of St. Paul that "he who does not govern his household well is not worthy to govern the house of God," Holly ruled with an iron hand. He refused to allow his progeny, nine of whom were boys, "to plunge into disorder." It was his duty "to see to their instruction, to have them usefully occupied, to provide for their support and watch to keep them from the evil contagion of a corrupt society."[13]

He was determined above all to educate them. As he observed in 1873,

> I have nothing to bequeath to my children but the orthodox precepts of our apostolic religion, moral integrity, a useful education and industrious habits. I owe them this much under pain of being worse than a heathen and a pagan and of being in danger after having preached to others, to leave my own to become castaways.

During the children's early years Holly and his second wife, Sarah, instructing only in English, taught them spelling, writing, grammar, geography, science, mathematics, and music. The older sons also studied Latin and Greek. All were taught by their mother how to cook, all served "in regular order and gratuitously" as sexton (janitor) in the church, and all the boys were trained as shoemakers.[14]

Holly devoted much time and effort to securing advanced education for each of his sons. The bishop begged and borrowed enough in money and scholarships from churchmen in England and America to finance a process that extended from September 1875—when he took his two eldest boys, Theodore Faustin and Augustine, to the United States to school—to June 1900, when his youngest son, Robert, completed his studies in America. The scholastic achievements of these boys, children of a self-educated, impoverished black clergyman, bordered on the phenomenal, although Holly himself was not surprised. He expected them to succeed and then return to Haiti to become examples to the people of the Black Republic. Haiti would grow under the leaderships of his sons, "living epistles to be seen and read by all men."[15]

The two eldest sons, issue of the bishop's first marriage to Charlotte Ann Gordon, studied primarily in Haiti. Theodore Faustin prepared for the priesthood under his father's direction and then served under him for nearly twenty-three years as the loyal and hardworking associate minister of Holy Trinity Church. Augustine occasionally worked for his father as overseer of the farm school. He also taught in government schools. The seven younger sons all studied abroad, and six achieved advanced degrees. John Alfred Lee Holly graduated at the top of his class from Codrington College in Barbados, and went on to the General Theological Seminary in New York City. Alonzo Potter Burgess Holly studied four years in England and subsequently took a medical degree from New York Homeopathic College. Ambroise Theodosius Holly, the first Negro to graduate from the Massachusetts College of Pharmacy, also attained a medical degree at the University of Pennsylvania. Sabourin Holly studied dental surgery in Philadelphia. Louis Holly attended the Boston Conservatory of Music before becoming ill and returning to Haiti to teach. Arthur Cleveland Coxe Holly was awarded a medical degree from the University of Boston and a diploma as "oculist and aurist" from the New York Ophthalmic College. The youngest child, Robert A. Holly, received a degree in mechanical engineering from Pratt Institute.[16]

Once educated, the Holly children continued to distinguish themselves in their chosen occupations. With two exceptions, however, their religious enthusiasm never matched that of their father. Even John Alfred Lee Holly, who was trained to the priesthood, left active church work to seek "more financial remuneration" in a job with the Haitian government. The others generally worked for the government or conducted private medical practices. The four doctors, at their father's insistence, donated a portion of their time to serving the needs of the poor. The physicians prospered: in his seventieth year Holly observed that they had fine buggies, whereas he had never even owned a horse. The two children who displayed their father's zeal for the Episcopal Church were Theodore Faustin (d. 1903) and Grace Theodora, the only daughter who survived to adulthood. She was considered by her father to be the family's best scholar, but their poverty prevented her from studying abroad. She was also the child most interested in her father's church. Here again the situation was ironic, for Holly's church, like all Anglican churches, was dominated by men and offered Grace Theodora no role commensurate with her ability and enthusiasm. She at least was able to teach French at Tuskegee Institute in Alabama and become an authoress whose articles on Haiti were published in American Negro newspapers and magazines.[17]

Holly's children were, perhaps, his greatest success. Frustrated in many of his endeavors, he did leave Haiti a dynasty of well-educated professional men.

**XI**                          **The
                                Final
                                Thrust**


At the turn of the twentieth century an aging but still active Holly involved himself in both the infant Pan-African movement and in a call for renewed immigration to the Caribbean islands. He also made a last effort to secure from the American church a permanent endowment that would guarantee the continuance of the Orthodox Apostolic Church of Haiti after his death. Described by a church periodical as "a character in the true heroic mold," the bishop never abandoned his dreams for the black man.[1]


I


James Theodore Holly was constant all his life in his support for black nations. "History attests," he wrote in 1851, "that emigration and settlement beyond the operation of political disabilities . . . is the regenerative power of baptism politically to a denationalized people." Fifty years later he was still preaching the tenets of emigration to American Negroes, a group he considered "pariahs excluded from political, social and economic privileges and forever doomed to be mere hewers of wood and drawers of water." The black man who lived in America, or as part of a minority in any country, would never be recognized or ackowledged, he believed, as an integral part of a white nation.[2]

Holly did not hate white people. He loved black people more. The white man looked out only for himself, he felt, and the Negro should do likewise. Although hopeful of a change in racial attitudes, Holly always believed what he had written to Alexander Crummell in 1864, that "black men must hold up one another . . . for we have not much to expect from white men." Holly did encourage friendships with useful whites. He did want the Negroes of the world to emulate the "vim and vigor" exhibited by American whites in education and industry. And exhibiting both pragmatism and idealism he urged his fellow Haitians to do as he had done by sending their children to professional schools in the United States. Once educated, the new generation of black leaders would return to "more congenial fields and pass on their skills to their brethren in order to build up a politically and economically independent black nation."[3]

Despite the failure of the grandiose black emigration schemes of the 1850s and early 1860s, the movement never completely died away. At the urging of negrophile Edward Wilmot Blyden of Liberia, the American Colonization Society continued to send a trickle of black emigrants there. When Reconstruction ebbed in the South and racial prejudice failed to abate in the North, the number of American Negroes interested in emigration rose sharply. The secretary of the American Colonization Society noted in 1878 the eagerness of prospective emigrants in almost every state. In Charleston, South Carolina, the "Liberian Exodus Company," of which Martin R. Delany was secretary, reported 60,000 people ready for passage. And in Georgia a new leader, Henry M. Turner, had risen to rekindle the idea of African colonization. The "Back to Africa" movement dominated most of the space in black papers and other periodicals, but exhortations occasionally appeared for colonization in Haiti and its neighbor, Santo Domingo, "countries within easy reach of the United States by palatial steamship . . . and governed entirely by members of the race." Naturally, these efforts delighted the bishop of Haiti.[4]

In mid-1862, at a time when his own New Haven colony was foundering and the parent Haytian Emigration Bureau was about to close its doors forever, Holly had written confidently that his church—a new national church in Haiti— "would lay the solid foundation for a future emigration" of American Negroes to the Black Republic. Thirteen years later he spoke in more specific terms about emigration programs. He had come to visualize a broader base for the "solution of the [American] Negro problem," incorporating all of the West Indies. Holly wanted to revive the Blair plan of 1858, which had called for active participation by the United States government in securing homes in the Caribbean for American blacks. In October 1875 Holly spoke to a large group of Negroes in Washingon, D.C., on the subject of creating an independent West Indian confederacy "in which the Negro shall be the dominant factor, politically and otherwise." At the end of the nineteenth century Holly was a living link between the crusaders of the 1850s in support of emigration to Africa or the West Indies and the Pan-African movement. Pan-Africanism was, as one of its founders, W. E. B. DuBois, observed, an emotional and intellectual reaction of Negroes generated from the idea of "one Africa uniting the thoughts and ideas of all native people of the dark continent." It was not a clearcut political concept, but, in the words of a later student, an "ill-defined vague sentiment, a vision or a dream." This flexibility permitted the movement to attract black leaders from all over the world. Veterans such as Holly and young men such as DuBois could feel comfortable in supporting an organization based on a wish to see the Negro accepted in the modern world in real equality. For Holly the roots of Pan-Africanism stretched back to the National Emigration Convention of 1854.[5]

Twentieth-century Pan-Africanism may be said to have had its beginning when Sylvester Williams, a native of Trinidad who lived in London, formed the African

Association in 1897. An Association circular called for an increased feeling of unity and for friendly intercourse among all Negroes throughout the world to promote and protect the interests of all subjects, in all places, who claimed African descent. Response to the circular was sufficient to warrant a series of exploratory meetings looking toward a full-scale conference in London in 1900. Holly and many other black leaders throughout the world, including Henry M. Turner, Booker T. Washington, Alexander Walters, and W. E. B. DuBois of the United States, were invited to participate. Preparatory meetings were held in London in June 1899. Holly no doubt could have sat in on the planning sessions, but he was busy with church duties and too poor to attend. He may have sent, however, a letter with suggestions to be read at the meeting as he had done in 1851 when he was prevented from traveling to the North American Conference in Toronto.[6]

Twenty-four delegates assembled in London in July 1900 for a conference that broadened the work of the African Association and changed its name to Pan-African Association. Highlight of the sessions was an explanation by DuBois of the grievances of the race. Of special interest to the absent Holly was a speech by G. W. Christian that included a call for increased emigration in the Western Hemisphere. The Pan-African Association elected both central and regional officers, among them DuBois for the United States and Holly for Haiti. The next meetings were to be held in the United States in 1902 and two years later in Haiti.[7]

Like so many of the Negro conventions, conferences, and projects of the nineteenth century, the new Pan-African Association proved to be a short-lived organization existing only on paper. The meetings in the United States and Haiti never materialized. Feeble and premature as the effort was, it nevertheless marked a beginning of the Pan-African movement of the later twentieth century.

The work of the Pan-African Association in 1900, with its references to the blacks of the Western Hemisphere, stimulated Holly once more to encourage Caribbean emigration. In October 1901 the bishop wrote out in detail a "negro confederacy plan" and sent it to President Theodore Roosevelt. He received only a perfunctory reply from a presidential secretary. Next he submitted a shorter version of the plan to the managing editor of the New York *Journal*. The statement so impressed the editor that it was printed in all seventy-five papers of the Hearst Syndicate. Holly's article, "West Indies Confederacy for the Negro," bluntly declared that racial discrimination of epidemic proportions existed in all areas of the United States. He denounced as the "grossest stupidity" the belief of American whites that ten-million blacks and their descendants could ever be satisfied while excluded from all political, social, and civil privileges. He praised the "noble efforts" of Booker T. Washington and his "like-minded associates" and the results achieved by their agricultural and industrial schools. Yet he also criticized these same men for allowing their graduates to settle down in subservient, second-rate jobs in the United States. Haitians were "men of no such crouching servility." Only among them or in other Negro islands of the West Indies could American blacks find a "wide and more congenial field for their full and unstinted development."

Holly's plan for a West Indies confederacy, very simply put, called for the United States government, "in pursuance of the Monroe Doctrine," to purchase all European-held islands in the West Indies. The black inhabitants of the islands could then allow the United States to take a "hegemonic hand" in guiding the organization of a Negro confederacy. The purchase price of the islands would constitute a national debt of the confederacy to be paid off over many years. According to Holly, all sides would be satisfied. Black emigrants from America would be free and independent, and the confederacy would act as a "safety valve" by draining off the excess black labor force and relieving racial tension in the United States.[8]

Nothing ever came of Holly's plan. He was certainly not in a position to exert much influence in attracting attention to it. And he must have realized that, like their grandparents, the great majority of Negroes living in the United States of 1900, no matter what their everyday hardships were, preferred to stay at home.

## II

By the late 1890s the leadership of the board of managers of the Domestic and Foreign Missionary Society had fallen into the hands of younger men, notably Arthur Selden Lloyd and John Wilson Wood. Interest in the progress of Holly's church was now barely visible at the Church Missions House. Lloyd and Wood were concerned instead with teaching "American ways" and evangelizing souls in China, Japan, Africa, Brazil, Alaska, and Hawaii. After the triumphant Spanish-American War, the Philippines, Cuba, and Puerto Rico also became objects of their attention. These fields—not Haiti—received the ever-increasing missionary funds for building schools, hospitals, and cathedrals. To justify their parsimony toward the Orthodox Apostolic Church of Haiti, the board of managers pointed to the constant state of upheaval in the Black Republic and to the small number of communicants in Holly's church. The white bishop of Puerto Rico expressed privately what many churchmen believed—that "the incontrovertible fact of racial inheritance had to be taken into account." And because the leadership of the American church did not understand "brainy darkies" such as the bishop of Haiti, it chose, whenever possible, to ignore him.[9]

Holly did receive permission to come to the United States in the late summer of 1900 to undertake a strenuous and lengthy fund-raising campaign for his church.

On a visit to the Church Missions House he prepared several short brochures to be distributed to influential clergy and laymen. In them he explained the work he had done in Haiti and described the objectives he still hoped to achieve. "A Christmas Plea," the strongest of the pamphlets, made clear Holly's belief that the missionary operation in Haiti, despite past financial trouble, had been successful. He listed the annual expenditures of the missions in Africa, China, Japan, and Haiti, and the number of communicants and ordained missionaries in each field. These comparisons illustrated that his national church, "in spite of the very meager appropriations affected to the Haitian mission field," had surpassed her sister missions in relative achievements.[10]

Holly spoke before many church groups and conferred privately with countless bishops and clergy between August 1900 and April 1901, but he raised pledges of only $6,000 toward his goal of $25,000. His call went unheeded, and his campaign was ignored in Negro newspapers. Only in Baltimore did he receive a warm welcome from the Negro community, and that was due to the individual efforts of the Reverend George Bragg, Jr., rector of St. James Episcopal Church and editor of the *Church Advocate*.[11]

Holly arrived back in Port-au-Prince on April 12, 1902, to be feted at a gala reception and open house. He spent three months at home before resuming his campaign in the United States. This time he enjoyed being the ranch guest in Santa Barbara of a merchant he had known forty years earlier, and took pride in attending his first general convention as a bishop. Otherwise, the second try was even less successful than the first. Because of broken pledges, Holly departed for Haiti with barely $2,500 collected for church work.[12]

Shortly after this return to Haiti, which was to be his last, Bishop Holly received word from the Church Missions House that the associate secretary, Joshua Kimber, had been appointed the Haitian church's "official channel of communication to the United States." Lloyd and Wood were indicating to Holly that they were too busy with the more important missions—outposts filled with their personal friends—to devote any time or effort to the problems of the church in Haiti. Holly chose, however, to ignore the request that all mail from Haiti be directed to Kimber. Instead, he sent a long letter to General Secretary Arthur Lloyd that offered a plan to reform the "slip-shod" arrangements currently employed to support the mission work of the American church. Holly would have the regular appropriations augmented by a new, positive figure of endowments. The endowment, he suggested, should be $300,000 for each field, yielding an annual income of $12,000. Holly's plan was ignored.[13]

Holly had no thoughts either of retiring or of delegating any of his control over the Haitian church to his subordinates. His advancing years were as yet dealing gently with him. Although his hair, bushy eyebrows, flowing mustache, and short goatee had long since turned white, his frail figure, clothed in baggy suits, was still a familiar sight on the streets of Port-au-Prince. He announced to American officials in 1903 that "There may be at least ten years more of active labor in me." On occasion rheumatism, especially in his feet, flared up—"I have to tread as softly and lightly as walking on eggs"—but he refused to cancel his visitations into the wilderness areas of Haiti. He continued also to teach in the seminary and, periodically, to make the long and tiring journey to his lone missionary station in the Republic of Dominica.[14]

In his last years Holly concentrated his efforts on church work and concerned himself much less than he previously did with outside problems and issues. His letters no longer bemoaned the revolutionary turmoil in Haiti nor discussed racial problems in the United States. To the surprise of Joshua Kimber, he did not comment on the intervention of the United States in Dominica in 1905. He even seemed oblivious to the growing controversy in the American church over the expanding role of Negro clergy and bishops.[15] Communications between Holly and the Church Missions House were infrequesnt after 1907, and Haiti became more and more isolated from the American church.[16]

His dispatches to the American church in his later years were concerned chiefly with practical problems—or emergencies—experienced by the Haitian church. A three-day blaze in Port-au-Prince in July 1908 destroyed 1,200 buildings, among them Holy Trinity Church and the mission school house. The new rectory, situated several bloscks away from the other church property, was saved. Holly reported this latest catastrophe as "a direct deadly assault on the propagation of the gospel here, stirred up by the powers of darkness." Yet he announced that "we do not feel like *showing the white feather* by being discouraged and running away." To this news, received by telegraph, Lloyd made a well-intentioned if somewhat naive reply:

> I know what it [the loss of the church] means to you, but I hope you will not allow it to distress you unduly. It may be that it will stir the interest of the church in this country for the work you have given yourself so long and so faithfully, so that it may turn out to be a blessing in disguise. . . . My dear Bishop, you do not hear from us often, but I hope you know that our silence is never due to a lack of interest.

Lloyd went on to ask questions concerning the type of fire insurance the Haitian mission carried and the ability of the congregation to rebuild their church. Holly's response was brief. Church Missions House should know that foreign insurance companies would not issue coverage in Haiti. As to the congregation's wealth, "no members of our church are in cozy circumstances."[17]

After Lloyd's condolences no further action was taken in the United States with regard to the rebuilding of Holy Trinity Church until the December meeting of the board of managers. A perfunctory recommendation then passed, allowing the bishop of Haiti to issue an appeal for funds in American church newspapers. The plea met with scant success. Indeed, some American churchmen expressed doubt that further contributions should be made to rebuild a church so often destroyed.[18]

## III

Whatever his brave words, the fire of 1908 was in fact a severe setback to Bishop Holly. Nearly seventy-nine years old, he was at last slowing down his pace. His church service at five o'clock in the morning had been rescheduled to nine o'clock. He was becoming forgetful, and on occasion inadvertently overdrew his account or deleted names of his missionaries from the monthly salary list. As a result, and at the urging of his family, he reluctantly engaged his son John Alfred Holly as private secretary. Even with the latter's assistance the bishop's letters to the United States became infrequent and brief, and his skimpy annual report to the board of managers for the year 1909 was a far cry from the many-paged documents of former years. But he tried to remain active. A theme repeated in several of his sermons in 1909 was that of the old Protestant ethic: "Hard work and thrift pay dividends." Ironically, he could hardly offer his own career as a testimony in any material sense to that philosophy. After fifty-four years in the ministry he was literally penniless, and his Haitian church was still struggling to survive.[19]

There were joys and honors, to be sure. The board of managers recommended for the Haitian appropriation of 1909–1910 a record budget of $10,280. In October 1909 his family and friends, under the direction of his daughter Grace Theodora, celebrated the bishop's eightieth birthday at a solemn service of thanksgiving. A month later, in an unprecedented gesture, General Antoine Simon, president of the Republic of Haiti, accompanied by his entire cabinet, attended a commemorative service to celebrate completion of a thirty-fifth year of Holly's episcopate.[20]

During the last eighteen months of his life, however, Holly lost control of his personal affairs and of the Orthodox Apostolic Church of Haiti. A commission composed of his sons, John Alfred, Arthur C., and Robert, joined by Pierre Jones, Alexandre Battiste, and others, wrested active leadership of the church from their stubborn bishop. The commission browbeat the enfeebled Holly into "reluctantly" relinquishing his absolute control over mission affairs. At a special meeting in the rectory, Dr. Arthur C. Holly read to his father a paper taxing him with having paralyzed the initiative of the Haitian church. Acting upon the advice of Arthur Holly, the board of managers in New York City had previously relieved Bishop Holly of all financial responsibility and directed the treasurer to send the monthly drafts directly to the address of each missionary in Haiti. Then the commission moved to solidify its control over the Haitian church, and in so doing evinced resentment of the bishop's strong rule. To Bishop O. W. Whittaker, a member of the overseeing committee on Haiti, Arthur wrote:

> We are more convinced of a better future now that the Bishop has at last given us liberty to act. Church matters are discussed freely and decisions are taken by a group of men well intentioned, whereas before everything and anything was as the Bishop wanted it—I dare say he was not always right.[21]

Gradually, as the months of 1910 slipped by, the bishop's memory failed so markedly that he was able to do very little church work. Although forbidden by his son and doctor, Arthur, to leave the house, he continued to carry money to the poor. Often he fainted in the streets and had to be carried into a private home to be revived. On March 3, 1911, he took to his bed for the last time. Ten days later, at a quarter to four in the morning, with his family and friends near the bedside, he died quietly in his sleep.[22]

In a special cabinet meeting held in honor of Holly, the president of Haiti declared the bishop "a great man who has done much good for this country." On March 15 over 2,000 people attended a five-hour funeral ceremony conducted by eleven clergymen. In the main address Holly's associate of many years, Charles E. Benedict, preached from II Timothy 4:8: "I have fought a good fight, I have finished my course, I have kept the faith." This text, according to Benedict, was eminently "applicable to the Bishop's earthly career and sure hope in the Lord." Another observer wrote: "No one remembers seeing such a funeral, the crowd that followed was immense—the sidewalks and balconies were crowded with people. . . . There was not a piece of mourning [cloth] left in town . . . Bishop Holly had cleaned them out."[23]

Holly's name had been all but forgotten by Negroes in the United States. His great contemporaries of antebellum America—Douglass, Langston, Delany, Garnet, and Crummell—had all preceded him to the grave. Yet his one loyal supporter in the United States, the Reverend George Bragg, refused to allow the bishop's death to go unnoticed. He eulogized Holly in the *Church Advocate* and arranged and conducted a memorial service in Holly's old church, St. Luke's in New Haven. Present at this service were two survivors of Holly's New Haven colony.[24]

When James Theodore Holly died he had completed fifty years (lacking a few months) of missionary work in Haiti, and thirty-six years as the first Negro bishop in the American church. Yet the official announcement of his death in the *Spirit of Missions* was hollow at best, pointing out that the work in Haiti "has not prospered so greatly as was at one time hoped." The board of managers did nothing to commemorate his passing except strike his salary from the appropriations for 1911. Only the aged Joshua Kimber, who had corresponded with Holly for more than forty years, showed genuine concern. To Arthur he wrote that "the Bishop's death came to me as a personal affliction." And to Alonzo: "Your father was, as a shock of corn, fully ripe. I have deep sympathy with your mother. The dear old lady must be very lonely."[25]

# Epilogue

Was the life of James Theodore Holly one of frustration and failure? Upon reflection, "frustration" is applicable, but not "failure"—setbacks, yes; failure, no.

Holly exhibited in his personal makeup a very strong individuality and independence. He believed himself to be every inch a man, a black man, and a natural advocate for his race. Yet he was out of tune with the thinking of the free-Negro population in antebellum America. He was convinced that the only way the Negro of the United States could control his own destiny and be truly free was to leave the country; the majority of American blacks, including his friends and associates, preferred "to stay home" in hopes of a better tomorrow. They remained in the United States, while only Holly and a very few of his brethren successfully emigrated. Of all the prominent black spokesmen favoring emigration in the 1850s, Holly was the only one who left his homeland permanently.[1]

A resident in Haiti during the last half century of his life, Holly nevertheless maintained a keen interest in the black population he had left behind in America. And he never ceased to believe that those brethren would be far better off and far happier were they to follow his example, leave the United States, and settle in the Caribbean.

Holly stayed true to Haiti for over sixty years. He refused to entertain any thought that the country's lack of progress could be laid at the door of racial inferiority. Instead, he found scapegoats in Haiti's colonial background, the brutal war for independence, the derisive attitude of the outside world, the failure of popular education, and the oppressive yoke of Roman Catholicism. He believed that the potential for greatness was present in Haiti, and that his national church, led by him and based on the Anglican religion, would help to speed the Black Republic toward her promise.

When Holly arrived in Haiti in 1861 he was the lone Episcopal priest on an island previously untouched by that denomination. Thirteen years later, when he was consecrated bishop of the Orthodox Apostolic Church of Haiti, his native staff had grown to six priests and four deacons, who served eighteen scattered missionary stations and nearly one-thousand persons—of whom 250 were communicants. During subsequent decades the rate of growth was slow. The meagerness of funds from the United States for church work in Haiti and the unstable living conditions that prevailed throughout the Black Republic in Holly's lifetime frustrated the work of his church. The total membership of the Orthodox Apostolic Church of Haiti in 1911 was barely two-thousand souls, ministered to by twelve priests and two deacons in twenty-six stations.[2]

Underlying these statistics were substantial achievements. Holly's was the first autonomous national church established under Anglican auspices outside an English-speaking area. His accomplishment was to be emulated all over the world. To be sure, most of his plans for Haiti were never realized. But the simple fact of their being initiated established a precedent and opened the way for future works by the Episcopal Church in seeking to replace illiteracy, disease, and poverty in Haiti with education, health, and financial security.[3]

Holly expected and ardently desired the Republic of Haiti to become a "strong, powerful, enlightened and progressive Negro nationality," an example to blacks throughout the world. This goal was never achieved, nor even approached, but the continuous struggle toward it was the source of his strength, and ultimately his salvation.[4]

# Notes

## I    Steps to the North

1
See Leon Litwack, *North of Slavery: The Negro in the Free States, 1790-1860* (Chicago: University of Chicago Press, 1961).

2
This genealogical information has been drawn from the scattered, and at times inaccurate, recollections of Bishop Holly, from the bishop's son, Alonzo Potter Holly, and from interviewers of the bishop. The register certifying the 1772 manumission was destroyed in the St. Mary's County Courthouse fire in 1831. Holly's personal collection of the original documents vanished during the burning of Port-au-Prince in 1888. See New York *Sun*, November 1, 1896; James Theodore Holly, *Facts About the Church Mission in Haiti* (New York: Thomas Whittacker, 1896), p. 6; Alonzo Potter Holly, *God and the Negro* (Nashville: National Baptist Board, 1937), p. 153; "Letters to the Editor," *Journal of Negro History* VIII (November 1923): 454.

3
Holly, *Facts About the Church Mission in Haiti*, p. 6; Constance M. Green, *The Secret City* (Princeton: Princeton University Press, 1967), p. 15; Letitia Woods Brown, *Free Negroes in the District of Columbia, 1790-1846* (New York: Oxford University Press, 1972), p. 6.

4
Congress also systematically shut out free-black labor whenever any new public work programs were inaugurated in the District. Dorthy Provine, "The Economic Position of Free Blacks in the District of Columbia," *Journal of Negro History* LVIII (January 1973): 63; James Theodore Holly to William McClain, August 1, 1850, American Colonization Society Papers, Library of Congress.

5
Anne Royall, *Sketches of History, Life and Manners in the United States* quoted in Brown, *Free Negroes in the District of Columbia*, p. 129. See also Brown, pp. 134, 140; and Green, *The Secret City*, pp. 21, 37. The ordinance of 1836 was struck down by an enlightened Circuit Court decision. Provine, "The Economic Position of Free Negroes," p. 66.

6
The Snow Riot or "Snow Storm" was described after the Civil War as "an event that still stands vividly in the memory of all colored people who lived in this community at that time."—"Special Report of the Commissioner of Education on the Conditions and Improvement of Public Schools in the District of Columbia," *House Executive Document 315*, 41 Cong., 2 Sess., Vol 13, Serial 1427, pp. 65, 195, 201 (hereafter cited as "Spec. Rpt. Comm. Ed."). Young James had two older sisters, one who died during his youth, and Cecilia, who survived until 1853; and two brothers, Charles, who died shortly after James's birth, and Joseph, born in 1825.

7
It is conceivable that the Holly brothers, prior to entering Dr. Fleet's school, attended the Georgetown School "for colored boys" conducted by their place of worship, Holy Trinity Catholic Church. "Spec. Rpt. Comm. Ed.," pp. 65, 201, 213; "Bishop of Haiti," *Quarterly Message Concerning Church Missions* VI (October–December 1898), p. 35; Holly to George Flichtner, March 8, 1882, Domestic and Foreign Missionary Society: Haiti Papers, Archives and Historical Collections—Episcopal Church

(formerly the Church Historical Society), Austin, Texas (hereafter cited as Haiti Papers); Holly to John E. Bruce, January 1890, John E. Bruce Papers, Schomburg Collection, Harlem Branch, New York Public Library.

8

Joseph C. Holly, *Freedom's Offering* (Rochester: The Author, 1853); Holly, *Facts About the Church Mission in Haiti,* p. 6; "Spec. Rpt. Comm. Ed.," pp. 217–218. What is even more startling about the benevolent actions of the clergy of Holy Trinity is that the French priest who baptized Holly had been driven out of Haiti by black insurrectionists. Holly to William Langford, November 29, 1894, Haiti Papers.

9

Joseph C. Holly, *Freedom's Offering* (Rochester: The Author, 1853); "Spec. Rpt. Comm. Ed.," pp. 217–218.

10

Holly to McClain, August 8, 1850, American Colonization Society; Green, *The Secret City,* p. 37; District of Columbia Tax Books, Record Group 351, National Archives; "Spec. Rpt. Comm. Ed," p. 312. No evidence exists to reveal if the senior Holly considered emigrating from the United States. Some District blacks had previously gone to Liberia and the American Colonization Society officials actively recruited in Federal City. Brown, *Free Negroes in the District of Columbia,* p. 141.

11

James P. Hurley, "Walking Tour of the Museum of the City of New York: Bedford of Bedford Stuyvesant" (unpublished manuscript, Long Island Historical Society), p. 7; William J. Hearn and Edwin Nostrand, *Brooklyn Alphabetical and Street Directory for 1844/45* (Brooklyn: The Authors, 1845), p. 97; Hearne and Nostrand, *Brooklyn Alphabetical and Street Directory for 1845/46,* p. 107. Also see directories for 1846–1849 and *Frederick Douglass' Paper,* May 27, 1852.

12

Seth Scheiner, *Black Mecca* (New York: New York University Press, 1965), pp. 6, 22–24; Robert Ernst, *Immigrant Life in New York City, 1825-1863* (King's Crown Press, Columbia University, 1949), pp. 40–41, 67, 104. See also George Walker, "The Afro-American in New York City, 1827–1860" (Ph.D. diss., Columbia University, 1975).

13

Holly to McClain, June 25, 1850, American Colonization Society Papers; Holly to Joshua Kimber, January 7, June 13, 1884; Holly to Flichtner, March 8, 1882, Haiti Papers; Holly to William R. Whittingham, May 29, 1862, Maryland Diocesan Archives, Maryland Historical Society. Father Varela could always be found "in most of the bitter contests waged with non-Catholic assailants of the church." *The Tablet* (Brooklyn), December 12, 1908. Bertram Wyatt-Brown, *Lewis Tappan and the Evangelical War Against Slavery* (Cleveland: Case Western Reserve Press, 1969), p. 237. Tappan habitually paid low wages to all his employees.

14

Joseph C. Holly to the editor, *North Star,* February 18, 1848.

15

Seventh U.S. Census, 1850, Manuscript Returns of Schedule I, Free Inhabitants, for Burlington, Vermont; Holly to Flitchner, March 8, 1882, Haiti Papers. According to James, his family had a "hereditary predisposition" to consumption. Holly to McClain, August 8, 1850, American Colonization Society Papers.

16

Joseph C. Holly to the editors, *Voice of the Fugitive,* September 23, 1852; *North Star,* August 3, 1849; *Frederick Douglass' Paper,* September 22, 1854.

17

David Blow to Floyd J. Miller, April 16, 1969, copy in author's possession; Burlington *Free Press,* April 29, 1851; Holly to Flitchner, March 8, 1882, Haiti Papers. In later years, from Haiti, Holly continued to keep in touch with Tappan and requested his financial help for the mission there. For example, see Lewis Tappan to Holly, June 15, 1865. Tappan Papers, Library of Congress, wherein Tappan writes: "Remember that your letters always give pleasure to your friend and brother Lewis Tappan."

18

Burlington *Free Press,* July 23, August 15, 19, 1851; April 4, 1852.

19

Frederic Bancroft, "The Colonization of American Negroes, 1801–1865," printed in Jacob E. Cooke, *Frederick Bancroft, Historian* (Norman: University of Oklahoma Press, 1957) p. 154. The best study

of the Society is by P. J. Staudenraus, *The African Colonization Movement, 1816-1865* (New York: Columbia University Press, 1961).
20
Joseph C. Holly to Henry Clay, *North Star*, February 1, 1850. Joseph's criticism of the Society grew. In 1852 he wrote that any black who supported the Colonization Society was "a traitor, compared with whom Benedict Arnold was a pure patriot and Judas Iscariot an exemplary Christian." *Frederick Douglass' Paper*, August 27, 1852.
21
A hydropathic practitioner used the water cure to treat diseases. One would apply to a patient copious and frequent amounts of water both internally and externally. Homeopathy was the act of curing by producing in healthy persons effects similar to the symptoms of the complaint of the patient. Holly to McClain, June 25, July 30, September 3, 1850; McClain to Holly, July 31, 1850; McClain to Joseph Tracy, August 14, 1850; American Colonization Society Papers. In his letter to Tracy, McClain requested that the agent "inquire about Holly and in your Yankee way, make us an opinion about him." For unknown reasons McClain did not answer Holly's final letter to the Society in early September. *North Star*, February 1, 1850.
22
Holly to McClain, June 25, 1850, American Colonization Society Papers; *North Star*, February 1, 1850.
23
Holly to McClain, June 25, 1850, American Colonization Society Papers; Holly to the editor, *Voice of the Fugitive*, May 7, 1851.

## II    Search for a Place: Canada

1
Fred Landon, "The Negro Migration to Canada After the Fugitive Slave Act of 1850," *Journal of Negro History* V (January 1921): 22–23.
2
Henry Bibb, *Narrative of the Life and Adventures of Henry Bibb, An American Slave* (New York: The Author, 1850), passim; Fred Landon, "Henry Bibb, A Colonizer," *Journal of Negro History* IV (October 1920): 438–442. Excellent biographical sketches of virtually every black emigrationist (including Henry Bibb) active between the American Revolution and the Civil War can be found in Floyd John Miller, *The Search for a Black Nationality* (Urbana: University of Illinois Press, 1975).
3
*Voice of the Fugitive*, January 1, February 26, 1851.
4
Ibid., May 7, 1851.
5
Ibid., January 1, 1851.
6
Ibid., June 4, 1851.
7
*Frederick Douglass' Paper*, July 31, 1851.
8
*Voice of the Fugitive*, July 30, August 27, 1851.
9
Ibid., September 24, 1851.
10
Ibid., September 24, December 3, 1851.
11
Ibid., February 26, 1852. This explanation did not appear in the March 11, 1852, issue, and the subsequent March 25, 1852, number has been lost.
12
Ibid., March 11, April 15, June 19, 1852. The rest of Holly's family soon left Vermont. His beloved sister Cecilia had died in February 1852, and his mother accompanied Joseph to Rochester, New York. Burlington *Free Press*, February 11, 1852.

13
*Voice of the Fugitive,* June 3, 17, July 17, 1852.
14
Ibid., July 1, 1852.
15
William M. and Jane H. Pease, *Black Utopia; Negro Communal Experiments in America* (Madison: Historical Society of Wisconsin, 1963), p. 17. This excellent study includes a detailed chapter on the Refugee Home Society. One of the sponsors of the Society was the American Missionary Association.
16
Ibid., p. 113. On Shadd see Harold B. Hancock, "Mary Ann Shadd: Negro Editor, Educator and Lawyer," *Delaware History* XV (April 1973): 187–194.
17
Ibid., p. 184; Samuel Ward to "Dear Friend," *National Anti-Slavery Standard,* January 20, 1853.
18
Holly to the editor, *Liberator,* March 4, 1853.
19
*Provincial Freeman,* March 24, 1853. No other issues were published in 1853.
20
*Frederick Douglass' Paper,* January 21, 1853. Holly's former patron, Lewis Tappan, was not so tactful. He assured Ward that his continued criticism of the Society would cause the American Missionary Association to oppose his proposed speaking tour of England; *Frederick Douglass' Paper,* April 29, 1853.
21
There is no evidence that the *Voice of the Fugitive* was subsidized in any way, but revenue from subscriptions and advertising must have been small indeed. It is not inconceivable that some financial support was received from outside the black community.
22
Joseph C. Holly to the editor, *Voice of the Fugitive,* August 26, 1852.
23
*Voice of the Fugitive,* August 12, 26, October 21, 1852.
24
Ibid., July 15, 1852; Robin Winks, *The Blacks in Canada* (New Haven: Yale University Press, 1971), pp. 145–146.
25
*Voice of the Fugitive,* July 1, 1852. Because Negro newspapers in Canada and the United States had often died in mid-year without refunding advance payments, many blacks refused to subscribe to any Negro newspaper. *Frederick Douglass' Paper,* April 8, 1853.
26
*Voice of the Fugitive,* March 15, 1853; *Provincial Freeman,* March 25, 1854. In the minds of Bibb and Holly the words "nationalistic" and "immigrationist" were interchangeable.
27
*Minutes and Proceedings of the General Convention of Colored Inhabitants of Canada, held in Amherstburg, C. W.* (Windsor: Bibb and Holly, 1853), pp. 2–14. Only thirty-three blacks were in attendance.

## III    Change in Direction

1
*Proceedings of the Colored National Convention* (Rochester, 1853); Bella Gross, "The First National Negro Convention," *Journal of Negro History* XXXI (October 1946): 436. The best overall analysis of the Negro convention movement is found in Howard H. Bell, *A Survey of the Negro Convention Movement, 1830-1861* (New York: Arno Press, 1969). For biographical information on Munroe (also spelled Monroe and Monro), see Floyd John Miller, *The Search for a Black Nationality* (Urbana: University of Illinois Press, 1975), pp. 146–148. On Whitfield, see Joan R. Sherman, "James Monroe Whitfield, Poet Emigrationist: A Voice of Protestant Despair," *Journal of Negro History* LVII (April 1972): 169–176.

2
*Arguments, Pro and Con, on the Call for a National Emigration Convention, to be held in Cleveland, Ohio, August 1854* (Detroit, 1854), pp. 3, 32–33.

3
*Provincial Freeman,* June 28, 1855.

4
*Eighteenth Annual Report of the Superintendent of Public Schools of Buffalo* (Buffalo: Clapp, Mathew and Co., 1854), p. 23.

5
*Frederick Douglass' Paper,* December 8, 1854. Douglass actively opposed emigration and he made it a policy not to print comments favoring the movement. See statement in *Frederick Douglass' Paper,* December 8, 1854.

6
*Proceedings of the National Emigration Convention of Colored People held at Cleveland, Ohio, the 24th, 25th, and 26th of August 1854* (Pittsburgh: A. A. Anderson, 1854), pp. 16–18, 31–32.

7
Delany did go to Africa to explore the Niger Valley in 1859. When the Civil War began he abandoned his emigration ideas to stay home and work for the Union. After the war he was active in the Reconstruction politics of South Carolina. At the twilight of his career he turned once more to Africa and endorsed emigration to Liberia. See Victor Ullman, *Martin R. Delany, the Beginnings of Black Nationalism* (Boston: Beacon Press, 1971); and Cyril E. Griffith, *The African Dream: Martin R. Delany and the Emergence of Pan-African Thought* (University Park: The Pennsylvania State University Press, 1975).

8
*Proceedings . . . 1854 Convention,* pp. 17, 76–77. Holly's description of the secret sessions is found in his letter quoted in John Cromwell, *The Negro in American History* (Washington: The American Negro Academy, 1914), pp. 43–44.

9
New York *Sun,* November 1, 1896; *Voice of the Fugitive,* September 7, 23, October 7, December 2, 1852; *Ancient Landmark* III (February 1854): 107; *Frederick Douglass' Paper,* January 5, 1855; Joseph Holly to the editor, ibid., October 28, 1853.

10
Holly, *Facts About the Church Mission in Haiti,* p. 6.

11
Holly to John H. Hopkins, March 5, 1868, Bishops Papers, General Theological Seminary. Paradoxically, the bishop of Vermont, besides being an outspoken advocate of slavery, was much concerned with keeping Episcopalianism "pure" Caucasian. He believed that God had meant for blacks to be servants of the white race and if Negroes were legally and socially free it would put them in a false position. See John H. Hopkins, *View of Slavery* (New York: W. I. Pooley and Co., 1864); *Voice of the Fugitive,* June 7, 1852.

12
Holly to Hopkins, March 5, 1868, Bishops Papers, General Theological Seminary; Holly to Arthur C. Coxe, September 22, 1864, Haiti Papers; George E. Bragg, Jr., *History of the Afro-American Group of the Episcopal Church* (Baltimore: Church Advocate Press, 1922), pp. 117, 192; William C. Munroe, *A Brief History of St. Matthews Protestant Church* (Detroit, ca. 1856), p. 1.

13
Horace Hill, Jr., to Samuel Denison, May 5, 1855; Holly to Denison, August 1, 1855, Haiti Papers; George F. Bragg, Jr., *Men of Maryland* (Baltimore: Church Advocate Press, 1914), p. 80; *Provincial Freeman* October 13, 1855. In addition to Haiti, Holly was commissioned to Jamaica, St. Thomas, Nassau, Martinique, Guadeloupe, and Central America. Holly to Martin R. Delany, January 29, 1861, in *Anglo-African,* February 9, 1861. Munroe had previously served in Haiti from 1835–1838 as a Baptist missionary. Miller, *Search for a Black Nationality,* p. 147.

14
Holly to Denison, August 1855; New York *Tribune,* September 5, 1855; Holly to Delany, January 29, 1861, in *Anglo-African,* February 9, 1861; *North Star,* June 13, 1850; Gustave D'Aleux, *Soulouque and His Empire* (Richmond: J. W. Randolph, 1861).

15
Holly to Delany, January 29, 1861, in *Anglo-African,* February 9, 1861; *Provincial Freeman,* October 13, 1855; James Theodore Holly to Frank P. Blair, Jr., January 30, 1858, in Blair, *The Destiny of the Races of this Continent, with Appendix* (Washington, D.C.: Buell and Blanchard, 1859), pp. 36–37; Miller, *Search for a Black Nationality,* p. 163.
16
Holly to Denison, August, September 10, 1855, Haiti Papers. The report is appended to the letter.
17
*Churchman,* November 1, 1855; *Church Journal,* November 8, 1855; Holly to Joshua Kimber, December 10, 1877, Haiti Papers.
18
James Theodore Holly, *Vindication of the Capacity of the Negro Race for Self-Government and Civilized Progress* (New Haven: Afric-American Printing Co., 1857), pp. 5, 42–43. The lecture is reprinted in Howard H. Bell, ed., *Black Separatism and the Caribbean* (Ann Arbor: University of Michigan Press, 1970).
19
Ibid., p. 46.
20
Holly to William Hare, February 28, 1872; Gregory T. Bedell to Denison, November 13, 1855, Haiti Papers. Denison to Holly, November 22, 1855, Foreign Committee Correspondence Sent; Minutes of the Foreign Committee, December 27, 1853; September 25, October 1, 1855; October 28, 1856. Bedell had written Denison: "I am not in favor of establishing it [Haiti] as a mission under his [Holly's] direction."
21
*Journal of the Annual Convention of the Protestant Episcopal Church in the Diocese of Connecticut,* 1856, p. 15; "The Bishop of Haiti," *Quarterly Message Concerning Church Missions* VI (October–December 1898): 35.
22
The Diocese of Connecticut, acting upon letters from the Reverend Samuel V. Berry, a black Brooklyn priest, Munroe, and two laymen from St. Luke's, appointed Holly rector. Miller, *Search for a Black Nationality,* p. 165. Robert A. Warner, *New Haven Negroes, A Social History* (New Haven: Institute of Human Relations, 1940), p. 86; Bragg, *History of the Afro-American Group of the Episcopal Church,* pp. 106–107. In 1850 the vestry, short of funds, had voted to "temporarily dispense with public worship." St. Luke's Church, Minutes of Meetings, April 24, 1850.
23
St. Luke's Church, Minutes of Meetings, October 14, 1856; February 8, April 25, 1858; April 1, 1861; Warner, *New Haven Negroes,* p. 88; *Journal of the Diocese of Connecticut* (1856): 51, (1859): 53.
24
*Provincial Freeman,* May 16, 1856. The few surviving manuscripts of Munroe exhibit faulty prose and punctuation and are not up to the level of the published announcement. See his letters in Personnel File, Archives of the Protestant Episcopal Church.
25
Holly, *Vindication of the Capacity of the Negro Race,* p. 3; *Calendar,* August 16, 1857; *Church Journal,* July 31, 1856; William Wells Brown, *The Black Man, His Antecedents, His Genius, and His Achievements* (New York: Thomas Hamilton, 1863), p. 274.
26
Mary Shadd Carey's new husband, George Carey, was a friend of Holly who had a past history of interest in emigration. More important, probably, in Mrs. Carey's change of mind was increased racial discrimination in Canada and a hope that the impoverished *Provincial Freeman* might increase its circulation by becoming the official paper of the emigration movement. See *Provincial Freeman,* July 5, 1856.
27
*Provincial Freeman,* November 25, 1856. Other produce and free labor movements initiated or supported by Negroes of America and Liberia had been meant to harm the slaveholding South, and all had failed. See Richard K. McMaster, "Henry Highland Garnet and the African Civilization Society." *Journal of Presbyterian History* XLVIII (Summer 1970): 99–100.

28
The Afric-American Printing Company did publish in 1857 Holly's *Vindication of the Capacity of the Negro Race.*
29
*Provincial Freeman,* November 25, 1856; Martin R. Delany, "Official Report of the Niger Valley Exploring Party," in Howard H. Bell, ed., *Search for a Place* (Ann Arbor: University of Michigan Press, 1969), p. 36; Holly to Delany, January 29, 1861, in *Anglo-African,* February 9, 1861.

# IV     Search for Allies

1
Holly to Martin R. Delany, January 29, 1861, in *Anglo-African,* February 9, 1861.
2
"Spec. Rpt. Comm. Ed.," pp. 328, 334; *Annual Report of the Board of the First School Society for 1856* (New Haven: T. J. Stafford, 1856), p. 31; *Annual Report of the Board of Education of New Haven City School District for 1858* (New Haven: T. J. Stafford, 1858), p. 21; *Annual Report,* 1859, p. 19; Warner, *New Haven Negroes,* p. 75. Gilman's report is made perhaps the more flattering by his disposition to the intellectual quality of Negroes and to see the "distinction between the two races . . . as permanent." See Daniel Coit Gilman, *The Launching of a University and Other Papers* (New York: Dodd, Mead and Co., 1906), p. 338.
3
*Anglo-African,* October 1, 1859.
4
*American Freemason* ser. 2, IV (December 1859): 468; *Anglo-African,* January 26, 1860.
5
Apparently the Society held an annual meeting each summer between 1856 and 1859. No records remain from 1856 and 1858, when the sessions were held in Detroit. In 1857 and 1859 the Society met in New Haven. *Calendar,* August 22, 1857; *Anglo-African,* October 22, 1859.
6
Ibid.
7
C. C. Trowbridge to Samuel Denison, November 15, 1858, H. P. Baldwin to Denison, November 13, 1858, Haiti Papers; William C. Munroe to Denison, November 13, 1859, Personnel Folders, Domestic and Foreign Committee, September 15, 1859. After Munroe secured a promise of aid from the New York Colonization Society, the foreign committee gave him $200 to "facilitate his purpose to emigrate to Liberia and to give himself to missionary work in that country." But they deferred his appointment "for future consideration." Munroe went to Liberia but fell ill immediately upon landing and died six weeks later. His wife and two children later returned to the United States. Munroe himself reportedly was planning to return when he died. Holly eulogized Munroe at Masonic funeral rites in New Haven in April 1860. Foreign Committee Minutes, May 3, 1859; Munroe to Denison, October 6, 1859, Personnel Folders, Domestic and Foreign Missionary Society, Church Historical Society; *Anglo-African,* April 14, May 31, 1860.
8
Staudenraus, *African Colonization Movement,* p. 251; Frank P. Blair, Jr., *The Destiny of the Races of This Continent,* p. 34.
9
Holly to Frank P. Blair, Jr., January 30, 1859, in Blair, *Destiny of the Races,* pp. 34–37; William E. Smith, *The Francis Blair Family in Politics,* 2 vols. (New York: Macmillan Co., 1933), I: 443.
10
*Anglo-African,* October 1, 1859, April 28, 1869; Warner, *New Haven Negroes,* p. 117.
11
James Theodore Holly, "Thoughts on Hayti," *Anglo-African* I (1859): 185, 220, 241–243, 327–329.
12
Holly to Leonidas Polk, April 26, 1860, Polk Papers, Sterling Library, Yale University; *Spirit of Missions* XXIV (November–December 1859): 496; Minutes of the Foreign Committee, March 13, 1860; Holly to Denison, March 19, 1860, Haiti Papers.

13
Denison to Holly, March 29, 1860, Foreign Committee Correspondence Sent; Foreign Committee Minutes, March 27, 1860.
14
Holly to Polk, April 26, 1860, Polk Papers. Holly persuaded Bishop Williams to write, unsuccessfully, to Samuel Wilberforce, the Anglican bishop of Oxford, seeking English support for a mission in Haiti. "Extracts showing favorable disposition of the British Church towards the Church in Haiti," 1869, Haiti Papers.
15
*Anglo-African*, February 18, 25, July 7, 1860; *Church Advocate*, April 1911; *Douglass Monthly*, March 1, 1859; Eighth U.S. Census, Manuscripts Returns of Schedule I, Free Inhabitants, for New Haven, Connecticut, National Archives.
16
Holly to James Redpath, November 27, 1860, in *Anglo-African*, April 6, 1861.
17
James Redpath, "Notes on a Visit to Hayti," New York *Tribune*, June 25, 1859.
18
*Douglass Monthly*, May 1859; James Redpath, ed., *A Guide to Hayti* (Boston: Haytian Emigration Bureau, 1860), p. 9; "Invitation of Geffrard." in *Pine and Palm*, May 18, 1861; Call for Emigration, in *Pine and Palm*, July 17, 1862; Holly to Blair, January 29, 1859, in Blair, *Destiny of the Races*, pp. 34–37. There is no adequate biography of Redpath, but a good sketch by Alvin F. Harlow appears in *Dictionary of American Biography*, 21 vols. (New York: Charles Scribner's Sons, 1935–1958), XV: 443–444.
19
John W. Cromwell, *The Negro in American History* (Washington: American Negro Academy, 1914), p. 44; Holly to Delany, January 29, 1861, in *Anglo-African*, February 9, 1861.
20
Holly, "The Establishment of the Church in Hayti," *Calendar*, December 1, 1860. His canvassing of the parishes in the New Haven area to seek funds for a church building netted scant results. See *Calendar*, February 9, 1861; and *Anglo-African*, March 25, 1861.
21
Howard H. Bell, "Negro Nationality: A Factor in Emigration Projects, 1858–1861," *Journal of Negro History* XLVIII (January 1962): 43–53; *Douglass Monthly*, January 1859, January 1861; Redpath to Victorien Plésance, June 24, 1861, Redpath Letterbook, Schomburg Collection, New York Public Library.
22
Holly to Delany, January 29, 1861, in *Anglo-African*, February 9, 1861.
23
The best biographical sketch of Smith is his obituary in *Anglo-African*, December 22, 1865. Garnet, still an advocate of "limited" settlement in Liberia, had become a paid agent for the Haytian Emigration Bureau. *Anglo-African*, December 22, 1860; March 16, 1861. See also Joel Schorr, *Henry Highland Garnet* (Westport: Greenwood Press, 1975).
24
The "Smith clique" included George T. Downing, a long-time advocate of "Staying at home," and J. C. Pennington, a brilliant but erratic Presbyterian minister. Redpath to Plésance, May 26, 1861, Redpath Letterbook, Library of Congress; James McCune Smith to Holly, in *Anglo-African*, February 23, 1861; Holly to the editor, *Anglo-African*, February 16, 1861.
25
Redpath to Plésance, May 27, 1861, Redpath Letterbook, Library of Congress; *Anglo-African*, March 16, 1861.
26
Redpath to Plésance, July 1, 1861, Redpath Letterbook, Library of Congress; William Coopinger to R. R. Gurley, November 17, December 20, 1860, American Colonization Society Papers.
27
John Brown, Jr., to Redpath, March 25, 1861, in Redpath to Plésance, March 31, 1861, Redpath Letterbook, Library of Congress.
28
Holly to Smith, in *Anglo-African*, February 16, 1861, Holly, "Thoughts on Hayti," *Anglo-African* I (1859): 298–300, 327–329, 365–366. In 1804 Governor-General Dessalines issued an appeal for

American Negroes to come to Haiti. Few did. Later, between 1818 and 1824, the government of President Boyer pushed for American emigration. An agent was sent to New York to recruit, and during this six-year period over 13,000 American Negroes settled in Haiti. But internal difficulties on the island, the hostility of the natives, and the indolence of many of the settlers caused the enterprise to fail. Emperor Faustin Soulouque I had employed two agents in the mid-1850s to recruit "ignorant" black laborers to cultivate his estate. See *Niles Weekly Register,* October 17, 1818; July 1, 1820; February 17, 1821; July 23, 1824; *Information for the Free People of Color Inclined to Emigrate to Haiti* (New York: Samuel Wood and Son, 1824); Loring D. Dewey, *Correspondence Relative to the Emigration to Hayti of the Free People of Colour in the United States* (New York: Mahlon Day, 1824); Floyd J. Miller, *Search for a Black Nationality* (Urbana: University of Illinois Press, 1975), pp. 76–82; *Pine and Palm,* June 19, July 30, 1862.

29
Redpath to Plésance, June 8, July 1, September 7, October 1, 13, 1861; to Fabre Geffrard, July 20, 1861; to Alexander Tate, July 19, 1861; Redpath Letterbook, Library of Congress; Redpath to Auguste Elie, February 12, 1862, Redpath Letterbook, Schomburg Collection.

30
Only about a dozen families actually emigrated from New Haven proper. Redpath to Plésance, March 31, 1861, Redpath Letterbook, Library of Congress; *Anglo-African,* March 23, 1861.

31
Holly to Redpath, quoted in Redpath to Plésance, March 31, 1861; Redpath to Plésance, April 16, 1861, Redpath Letterbook, Library of Congress.

32
Redpath to Plésance, April 29, 1861, Redpath Letterbook, Library of Congress; New Haven *Daily Morning Journal and Courier,* April 25, 1861; *Pine and Palm,* June 8, 1861.

# V    The Battle for Survival

1
Ebenezer Bassett, *Haiti* (Washington, D.C.: Bureau of Republics, 1893), p. 3. In 1861 the Dominican Republic was called San Domingo.

2
James G. Leyburn, *The Haitian People,* 1941, rev. ed. (New Haven: Yale University Press, 1961). This sociological study remains the most perceptive work on Haiti. The author details the emergence of the Haitian caste system—a system that has endured since 1804. See also Robert I. Rotberg with Christopher C. Clague, *Haiti: The Politics of Squalor* (Boston: Houghton Mifflin, 1971).

3
Holly to William Hare, May 30, 1872, Haiti Papers.

4
Holly to the editor, *Calendar,* July 6, 1861. The small number of emigrants from New Haven is indicative of the long antiemigration tradition in that city. See undated letter (ca. 1855) of Amos G. Beman in Beman Scrapbook, Beinecke Library, Yale University. For an elaboration of the difficulties experienced by the *Madeira* in clearing port see Redpath to Elie, May 6, July 1, 1861, Redpath Letterbook, Library of Congress.

5
Holly to Captain Morton, May 29, 1861, in *Pine and Palm,* August 3, 1961; *Pine and Palm,* June 22, 1861; Simpson, *Six Months in Port-au-Prince* (Philadelphia: George S. Ferguson Co., 1905), p. 75.

6
*Pine and Palm,* November 9, 1861; September 4, 1862.

7
Holly to Joshua Kimber, November 6, 1908, Haiti Papers; Holly to the editor, *Calendar,* June 14, July 17, 1861; *Pine and Palm,* July 13, 1861.

8
Letter to Jean Baptiste Drouillard, June 15, 1803, Haiti Collection, Rare Books Room, Boston Public Library; John Mercer Langston, *From the Virginia Plantation to the National Capitol* (Hartford: American Publishing Co., 1894), p. 367; *Pine and Palm,* July 13, 1861.

9
*Pine and Palm,* April 14, 1862. Publication of the *Anglo-African* had been resumed by Robert Hamil-

ton, brother of the paper's founder, with the financial support of James McCune Smith and in violation of a promise to Redpath. For critical comments on Haiti, see *Anglo-African,* August 10, 1861;
March 1, 1862.

10
*Anglo-African,* August 31, 1861.

11
Holly to the editor, *Pine and Palm,* August 24, September 28, 1861; May 29, 1862; Warner, *New
Haven Negroes,* pp. 31–32; Holly to "Chyrsa," August 17, 1903, Connecticut Diocesan Archives; St.
Luke's Parish Records, 1845–1885.

12
*Anglo-African,* August 31, September 7, 1861; Holly to the editor, *Pine and Palm,* August 24, September 7, 28, 1861; Redpath to Plésance, July 20, 1861, Redpath Letterbook, Library of Congress.

13
*Anglo-African,* October 5, 1861. Mrs. Munroe and her two children had accompanied her husband to
Africa in 1859, had returned to the United States after his death, then had traveled with Holly to Haiti.
She arrived back in the United States in October 1861. *Pine and Palm,* September 25, 1861; January 2,
1862; Redpath to Plésance, October 17, 1861, Redpath Letterbook, Library of Congress; Redpath to
Elie, May 21, 1862, Redpath Letterbook, Schomburg Collection.

14
*Anglo-African,* August 31, October 5, 1861; *Pine and Palm,* December 21, 1861.

15
Holly to the editor, October 28, 1861, *Pine and Palm,* December 21, 1861.

16
Samuel V. Berry to Holly, January 16, 1862, in *Anglo-African,* February 1, 1862; *Anglo-African,* October 19, 1861; January 18, 25, April 26, 1862.

17
*Pine and Palm,* August 3, 17, 1861; B. Ashley to the editor, November 12, 1861, in *Pine and Palm,*
November 6, 1861.

18
Holly to Berry, January 15, 1862, in *Anglo-African,* February 22, 1862; Holly to the editor, *Calendar,*
February 22, 1862; Holly to Mary E. Bibb Cary, August 6, 1862, in *Pine and Palm,* September 4, 1862;
Holly to Hare, May 30, 1872, Haiti Papers.

19
Holly to Geffrard, June 15, 1861, in *Pine and Palm, August 31, 1861; Pine and Palm,* July 3, 1862.

20
Holly to the editor, June 14, 1861, in *Church Journal,* July 17, 1861; Prince T. Rogers to the editor,
*Anglo-African,* September 7, 1861.

21
Holly to Hare, May 30, 1872, Haiti Papers; Holly to Cary, August 6, 1862, in *Pine and Palm,* September 4, 1862. Schemes by Redpath to reinvigorate the emigration movement, including a proposal to
ship recently freed slaves to Haiti, floundered. By the early autumn of 1862 the *Pine and Palm* had
ceased publication and the Haytian Emigration Bureau closed its doors forever. Fewer than 2,000
blacks had emigrated to Haiti. For a fuller description of the Bureau's work see Willis D. Boyd, "James
Redpath and American Negro Colonization in Haiti, 1860–1862," *The Americas* XII (October 1955):
176–182; and Floyd John Miller, *Search for a Black Nationality* (Urbana: University of Illinois Press,
1975), pp. 246–247.

22
Holly to Cary, August 6, 1862, in *Pine and Palm,* September 4, 1862; *Journal of the Diocese of Connecticut* (1862): 52.

23
Holly, *Facts About the Church Mission in Haiti,* p. 11; Holly to William Langford, October 25, 1890,
Haiti Papers; Holly to editor, *Calendar,* August 3, 1862.

24
Holly, *Facts About the Church Mission in Haiti,* p. 11; *Calendar,* January 4, June 21, 1862; Foreign
Committee Minutes, September 9, 1862; *Journal of the Great Convention* (1862): 125. The manuscript Minutes of the Foreign Committee reveal that the subject of how to cut operating expenses, in
the face of a 40 percent reduction of receipts, dominated the discussion of nearly all meetings during
the Civil War.

25
American Church Missionary Society, *Report,* 1860, pp. 8–13, 18–20; Heman Dyer, *Recollections of an Active Life* (New York: Thomas Whittaker, 1890), pp. 216–217. A brief but lucid discussion of the division between the two missionary societies is found in James T. Addington, *The Episcopal Church in the United States* (New York: Charles Scribner's Sons, 1951), pp. 152–163. For a more detailed analysis see George E. DeMille, *The Catholic Movement in American Episcopal Church* (Philadelphia: Church Historical Society, 1941).
26
Dyer, *Recollections of an Active Life,* p. 297; Charles T. Tyng, *Life of Stephen H. Tyng* (New York: E. P. Dutton and Co., 1890), pp. 338–340; Minutes of the Executive Committee of the American Church Missionary Society (hereafter abbreviated ACMS), November 3, 1862, February 1863; ACMS, *Report,* p. 24; Holly to George Whipple, November 11, 1862; American Missionary Association Papers, Fisk University.
27
Minutes of the Executive Committee of ACMS, May 1863.
28
Holly considered Haiti his permanent home and he referred to the United States as "your country." Holly to Denison, February 23, 1866; to Joshua Kimber, September 23, 1884, Haiti Papers.
29
Holly to Denison, February 23, 1866, Haiti Papers.
30
ACMS, *Report,* 1863, p. 15; Holly to Denison, February 23, 1866, Haiti Papers; Holly to editor, *Church Journal,* December 30, 1863; *Journal of the Diocese of Connecticut* (1864): 69.
31
ACMS, *Report,* 1864, pp. 10–16.
32
Ibid.
33
Lee's recommendation that Holly be paid his salary in gold had been approved. Holly to Denison, February 23, 1866; to Arthur C. Coxe, September 23, 1864, Haiti Papers; Minutes of the Executive Committee of the ACMS, February 6, 1864.
34
*Anglo-African,* August 1, 1863; Holly to Edward Anthon, November 30, 1865; to Denison, February 26, 1866, Haiti Papers.
35
Minutes of the Executive Committee of the ACMS, November 21, December 5, 1864; April 3, 1865; Holly to Hare, May 30, 1872; to Denison, February 26, 1872, Haiti Papers; Dyer, *Records of an Active Life,* p. 218.
36
Minutes of the Executive Committee of the ACMS, November 6, 1865; Holly to Denison, January 19, February 23, 1866, Haiti Papers.

## VI     The Continuing Struggle

1
*Church Advocate,* September 1921.
2
Herman Batterson, *A Sketch Book of the American Episcopate* (Philadelphia: J. B. Lippincott, 1884), pp. 155–156; George Burgess, *Last Journal of the Right Reverend George Burgess, D.D.* (Boston: E. P. Dutton and Co., 1866), p. 61; Holly to Denison, April 21, 1866, Haiti Papers.
3
Burgess, *Last Journal,* pp. 63–64.
4
Ibid., pp. 67–68.
5
Holly to Denison, April 21, 28, June 6, 1866, Haiti Papers.

6
George Burgess to Denison, March 19, 1866; Holly to Denison, April 28, June 26, 1866; Mrs. George Burgess to Denison, May 1866; Lee to Denison, June 9, 1866, Haiti Papers; Denison to Holly, May 22, 1866; H. M. Morrell to Lee, September 1866, Foreign Committee Correspondence Sent; Burgess, *Last Journal*, pp. 72, 80.

7
*Calendar,* June 2, 1866; Holly to Denison, June 25, 1866, Haiti Papers; Denison to Holly, December 24, 1866, Foreign Committee Correspondence Sent.

8
Holly to Denison, September 6, 1866; Lee to Denison, September 5, 1866; Pierre E. Jones, memorandum of interview with John W. Wood, March 28, 1911, Haiti Papers.

9
Lee to Denison, September 23, 1867, Haiti Papers. A translation of the *Registre* is attached to this letter.

10
Lee to Morrell, September 23, 1868, Haiti Papers; Holly to John Henry Hopkins, May 5, 1868, Bishops Papers, General Theological Seminary; Foreign Committee Minutes, February 6, 1868; Morrell to Holly, February 7, 1868, Foreign Committee Correspondence Sent.

11
Holly to Lee, February 3, 1868, Haiti Papers.

12
Lee to Morrell, March 12, 1868, Haiti Papers.

13
Holly to Hopkins, March 5, 1868, Bishops Papers, General Theological Seminary; Holly to Denison, September 27, 1868, Haiti Papers.

14
Holly to Benjamin Smith, June 19, 1869; Smith and Lee to Holly, July 3, 1869, Haiti Papers.

15
Extracts showing favorable disposition toward the church in Haiti, 1869, Haiti Papers; Lee to Denison, March 23, 1870, Haiti Papers.

16
Holly to Denison, November 9, 1866; July 1, 1870; to Richard Duane, June 28, 1873, Haiti Papers; Holly, Annual Report for Holy Trinity Parish, May 10, 1869, Haiti Papers.

17
Holly hoped to take over the missionary stations of the British Wesleyans when that Society withdrew from the island. But the Wesleyans decided to stay. Holly to Denison, February 5, 21, May 8, 1867, Haiti Papers; Holly, Annual Report for Holy Trinity Parish, May 10, 1869, Haiti Papers; Mark B. Bird to Benjamin Hunt, February 29, 1868, Haiti Collection, Rare Books Room, Boston Public Library.

18
Holly to Denison, April 7, 1870; Lee to Denison, April 13, 1870, Haiti Papers.

19
Denison to Holly, April 7, 1870, Foreign Committee Correspondence Sent; Lee to Denison, April 13, 1870, Haiti Papers; John Payne to Denison, April 25, 1870, Domestic and Foreign Missionary Society Papers: Liberia; Foreign Committee Minutes, June 6, December 19, 1870. Bishop Whipple did travel as far as Cuba before abandoning his visit to Haiti. Holly to Denison, August 1, 1866; Holly to Hare, April 12, 1871, Haiti Papers. Holly derived his belief in Satan's evils from Ephesians 6:12-20, especially 12: "For we wrestle not against flesh and blood but against *powers,* against the rulers of darkness of this world, *against spiritual wickedness* in high places."

20
Holly to Denison, April 13, 1867, J. N. Leger, *Haiti, Her History and Her Detractors* (New York: Neale Publishing Co., 1907), pp. 211-213; C. H. Hollister to William Seward, May 8, 1868, in U.S. Department of State, Despatches from U.S. Ministers to Haiti, 1862-1906, National Archives Microfilms M-82, Roll 3.

21
Hollister to Seward, May 29, August 11, 1868, Despatches, Roll 3; Holly to Denison, May 8, 1867, August 1, September 7, 1868, Haiti Papers.

22
James A. Padgett, "Diplomats to Haiti and Their Diplomacy," *Journal of Negro History* XXV (July 1940): 276; Ebenezer Bassett to Frederick Douglass, July 3, 1869, Frederick Douglass Papers, Library of Congress. See also Nancy Gordon Heinl, "America's First Black Diplomat," *Foreign Service Journal* 50 (August 1973): 20–22.
23
Holly to Denison, December 1, 1869, Haiti Papers.
24
Bassett to Douglass, July 3, 1869, Frederick Douglass Papers.
25
Holly to Denison, May 13, 1869; to James Aspinwall, February 7, 1870, Haiti Papers; Bassett to Hamilton Fish, January 15, 1870, Despatches, Roll 3.
26
Holly to George Flichtner, May 8, 1882, Haiti Papers.
27
Bassett was so popular in Haiti that at the completion of his official duties there he became the consular representative of the Haitian government in New York City.
28
John Hepburn to Lee, September 1, 1869, attached to Lee to Denison, September 29, 1869, Haiti Papers.
29
Lee to Denison, September 29, 1869, Haiti Papers; Denison to Holly, November 1, 1869, Foreign Committee Correspondence Sent.
30
Holly to Denison, December 1, 1869; Ebenezer Bassett to Foreign Committee, December 1, 1869, Haiti Papers; Foreign Committee Minutes, November 23, 1869.
31
Lee to Denison, February 8, 1870, Haiti Papers; Foreign Committee Minutes, February 21, 1870; Denison to Holly, March 5, 1870, Foreign Committee Correspondence Sent.

## VII    The Right Color

1
Holly to Joshua Kimber, December 30, 1879, Haiti Papers.
2
*Calendar,* January 11, 1862.
3
Holly to Alexander Crummell, April 22, 1864, Crummell Papers, Schomburg Collection. See also M. B. Akpan, "Alexander Crummell and His African 'Race Work': An Assessment of His Contributions to Liberia to Africa 'Redemption,' 1853–1873," *Historical Magazine of the Protestant Episcopal Church* XLV (June 1976).
4
Holly to Arthur C. Coxe, April 15, September 22, 1864, Haiti Papers.
5
Holly to Samuel Denison, September 7, 1868; January 8, 1871; to James Aspinwall, March 3, 1868, Haiti Papers.
6
Holly to Denison, March 2, 1871, Haiti Papers.
7
"Memorial from the P.E. Convocation in the Republic of Hayti, June 7, 1871," in Memorials to the General Convention, 1871, Archives of the General Convention, Church Historical Society; Minutes of the Foreign Committee, December 27, 1853; June 30, 1871; November 19, 1872; Charles C. Colmore to Arthur R. Gray, April 7, 1920, Domestic and Foreign Missionary Society: Puerto Rico Papers, Archives and Historical Collections—Episcopal Church.
8
Holly to William Hare, September 14, 19, October 11, 1871, Haiti Papers; *New National Era,* August 31, 1871.

9
Memorials and Petitions, Box 1, Archives of the General Convention; *Journal of the General Convention,* 1871, pp. 287–288; Holly to Hare, March 25, 1872, Haiti Papers; John Payne to Denison, August 12, 1869, Domentic and Foreign Missionary Society: Liberia Papers, Archives and Historical Collections—Episcopal Church; Holly to Crummell, April 22, 1864, Crummell Papers, Schomburg Collection. The author has read several letters of John Payne that reflect the bishop's prejudice against his black coworkers.
10
Holly to Hare, February 28, March 25, April 6, 25, 1872, Haiti Papers; Foreign Committee Minutes, April 27, 1872.
11
Holly to Hare, January 7, March 31, 1872, Haiti Papers.
12
Holly to Hare, December 21, 1871; February 28, May 31, 1872, Haiti Papers; Foreign Committee Minutes, April 22, 1872; Hare to Holly, July 5, September 3, 15, 1872, Foreign Committee Correspondence Sent.
13
Arthur C. Coxe, "Visitation of the Mission in Hayti," *Spirit of Missions* XXXVIII (May 1873): 321; Holly to Hare, May 30, November 29, 1872; January 3, 1873, Haiti Papers.
14
Coxe, "Visitation of the Mission in Hayti," pp. 321–325.
15
Henry C. Potter, *Reminiscences of Bishops and Archbishops* (New York: G. P. Putnam's Sons, 1906), p. 84; Coxe to William R. Whittingham, January 29, 1874, Maryland Diocesan Archives.
16
Holly to Richard Duane, May 29, July 1, September 25, October 14, December 6, 1873; May 31, 1875, Haiti Papers.
17
Holly to Duane, June 9, 23, October 18, 1873; St. Denis Bauduy to Duane, August 8, 1873, Haiti Papers; Holly to William Perry Stevens, June 30, 1873, Bishops Collection, Pierpont Morgan Library, New York City; Holly, *Facts About the Church in Haiti,* p. 23. Bishop Coxe once described Holly's library as "the best private library of French Theology" he had ever seen. "Bishop of Haiti," *Quarterly Message* VI, p. 35.
18
Mrs. James T. Holly to Duane, November 23, 1873; Bauduy to Duane, January 7, 1874; Holly to Duane, March 23, May 8, 1874, Haiti Papers; Holly, *Quarterly Report for 1874,* July 1874, Haiti Papers; Coxe to Whittingham, January 29, 1874, Maryland Diocesan Archives; Duane to Holly, March 6, 1874, Foreign Committee Correspondence Sent.
19
Foreign Committee Minutes, February 25, 1874; *Church Journal,* October 29, 1874; Holly to Alfred Lee, September 11, 1869; to Denison, July 18, 1870, Haiti Papers.
20
*Church Journal,* October 29, November 26, 1874; Kimber to Holly, July 1, 1884, Foreign Committee Correspondence Sent; Holly to Kimber, July 24, 1884, Haiti Papers. Law or no law, it would have been difficult for the House of Bishops to find a qualified and willing white candidate to fill the bishopric of Haiti. The Episcopal church had trouble securing a replacement for Bishop Payne of Liberia, and the man who finally accepted the job died six months after his arrival in Africa. *Spirit of Missions* XXXIX (December 1874): 768.
21
Holly to Duane, September 15, 1874; to Kimber, November 9, 1901, Haiti Papers; Holly, *God and the Negro,* p. 153.
22
*Church Journal,* October 29, 1874; *Spirit of Missions* XXXIX (December 1874): 769.
23
*Journal of the General Convention* (1874): 289.
24
Foreign Committee Minutes, November 25, 1874; Holly to Duane, November 25, 1874, Haiti Papers.
25
Holly to Duane, December 10, 1874, Haiti Papers.

26
Holly, *Triennial Report,* August 11, 1877, Haiti Papers.
27
Holly to Duane, February 20, 1875, Haiti Papers.
28
Holly to Duane, March 6, May 10, 1875, Haiti Papers; Cecil Halliburton, *A History of St. Augustine's College* (Raleigh: St. Augustine's College, 1937), p. 210.
29
Denison to "All Workers," December 24, 1875, Foreign Committee Correspondence Sent; Holly to Denison, January 20, 1876, Haiti Papers; Holly to Mrs. George Burgess, September 25, 1875, Connecticut Diocesan Archives; Holly to the Archbishop of Canterbury, April 10, 1876, Lambeth Library; William Bullock to Holly, March 22, 1875, United Society for the Propagation of the Gospel Papers, London; Holly to O. S. Prescott, February 23, 1876, Bishops Papers, General Theological Seminary; Holly to the editor, *Churchman,* March 18, 1876.
30
Duane to Holly, March 14, 1875, Foreign Committee Correspondence Sent; Holly to Kimber, October 8, 1878; June 27, 1884, Haiti Papers.
31
Foreign Committee Minutes, February 2, 1877; Kimber to Holly, October 3, November 22, 1877, Foreign Committee Correspondence Sent.
32
Holly to Kimber, October 3, 1877; December 30, 1879,; Holly to Denison, January 3, 1878; June 5, 1879, Haiti Papers.
33
Kimber to Holly, September 15, November 5, December 11, 1879; February 17, 1880, Foreign Committee Correspondence Sent.
34
"Foreign Relations: Hayti," Executive Documents, Forty-fifth Congress, 2nd session, I, no. 1, part 1 (Serial No. 1793), pp. 310–313; Holly to Kimber, June 8, 1877; February 16, 1898, Haiti Papers; Holly to Whittingham, June 21, 1877, Maryland Diocesan Archives.
35
Denison to Holly, May 14, 1878, Foreign Committee Correspondence Sent.
36
*Church Times,* July 5, 26, August 2, 1878; William Bacon Stevens, *The Lambeth Conference of 1878* (Philadelphia: The Author, 1878), p. 11.
37
William R. Curtis, *The Lambeth Conference, the Solution for Pan-Anglican Organization* (New York: Columbia University Press, 1942), pp. 7–13. Not until 1931 would the issue of race and worship be confronted. See *New York Times,* October 29, 1932.
38
Holly to Miss Cornelia Jay, May 7, 1886; to Kimber, December 21, 1878, Haiti Papers; Curtis, *The Lambeth Conferences,* p. 28.
39
Gregory T. Bedell, *The Canterbury Pilgrimage* (New York: Anson D. F. Randolph and Co., 1878), pp. 51–52, 165; Holly to Kimber, August 31, 1878; November 3, 1879; Holly, *Annual Report,* July 3, 1879, Haiti Papers; Holly to Bullock, July 16, 1878, United Society for the Propagation of the Gospel Papers; Holly, *God and the Negro,* p. 3; Edward W. Blyden to W. Coppinger, August 6, 1878, American Colonization Society Papers.
40
*People's Advocate,* April 19, 1879; Cromwell, *The Negro in American History,* p. 292; Bragg, *History of the Afro-American Group of the Episcopal Church,* pp. 195–197.

# VIII    Troubles on Every Side

1
Holly to Joshua Kimber, June 26, 1881, Haiti Papers.
2
Holly to Mrs. George Burgess, September 25, 1875, Connecticut Diocesan Archives; Holly to Richard Duane, August 14, 1875, Haiti Papers; *Journal of the Diocese of Connecticut* (1865): 56.

3
Holly to Kimber, September 5, November 4, 1879; January 26, 1881; to Alfred Lee, February 21, 1882, Haiti Papers; Holly, *Annual Report*, June 15, 1880, Haiti Papers.
4
Holly, *Annual Report*, June 15, 1880, Haiti Papers.
5
Kimber to Robert Stuart, March 16, 1881, Foreign Committee Correspondence Sent.
6
Holly to Kimber, March 10, 1881; Stuart to Kimber, March 26, 1881, Haiti Papers.
7
Bragg, *History of the Afro-American Group of the Episcopal Church*, p. 267; *Church Journal*, December 10, 1874; Holly to Lee, February 21, 1882; to William Langford, March 14, 1889, Haiti Papers.
8
Holly to Kimber, May 7, June 30, 1881, Haiti Papers; Holly, *Annual Report*, July 15, 1881, Haiti Papers.
9
Holly to George Flichtner, July 1, 1882; to Kimber, September 9, 1881, Haiti Papers.
10
John Robert Love to Holly, September 9, November 12, 1881, Haiti Papers; Foreign Committee Minutes, November 9, 1881. The original letter, containing Love's charges annotated with Holly's replies, was lost in the mail between New York and Wilmington, Delaware. Flichtner to Lee, March 14, 1881, Foreign Committee Correspondence Sent.
11
Holly to Love, November 12, 1881; to Arthur C. Coxe, December 28, 1881; Love to Holly, November 12, 1881; unsigned paper ca. December 1881, Haiti Papers.
12
Holly to Coxe, December 28, 1881, Haiti Papers.
13
Alexandre Battiste to Love, February 2, 1882; Battiste, St. Denis Bauduy, and Alex Heraux to Lee, February 6, 1882; Love to Battiste, February 6, 1882; Love to Lee, February 22, 1882, Haiti Papers.
14
Love to Lee, February 22, 1882, Haiti Papers.
15
Holly to Kimber, July 11, August 26, December 7, 1882. Love was found guilty of "(1) wilful, deliberate and malicious falsehood, . . . (2) wilful and deliberate violations of the rubric and canons of the church, . . . (3) having baptized a child after he had resigned, (4) wilful and deliberate violation of his ordinal vow by spreading division among the Church people—by inducing members to leave the Church, (5) refusing to obey the godly judgement of the Bishop." For the defendant's view of the proceedings, see J. Robert Love, *Is Bishop Holly Innocent?* (Port-au-Prince: T. M. Brown, 1885); and *Proof of Bishop Holly's Guilt* (Port-au-Prince: T. M. Brown, 1883).
16
Holly to Kimber, June 16, 1883, Haiti Papers.
17
Holly to Kimber, September 7, 1883, Haiti Papers. The preceding statement about missionary statistics is based upon extensive reading in the papers for Alaska, Greece, Haiti, and China of the Domestic and Foreign Missionary Society of the Protestant Episcopal Church in the United States.
18
Kimber to Holly, September 7, November 21, 1883, Foreign Committee Correspondence Sent; Holly to Kimber, August 8, October 16, November 22, 28, 1883, Haiti Papers; Foreign Committee Minutes, November 13, 1883; Lee and Coxe to Kimber, in Foreign Committee Minutes, December 11, 1883. John Robert Love did not immediately drop out of Holly's life. After his tour in the army he returned to Port-au-Prince, where he practiced medicine, preached, and "calumniated men of note" in articles and pamphlets. Holly reported that Love flirted with Catholicism, chased women, and made trouble. In 1887 he supposedly expressed an interest in denying all his past accusations against Holly. Two years later he was deported to Jamaica by the Haitian government "for fomenting domestic strife." Subsequently he published a book denouncing Romanism; criticized the Anglican bishop of Jamaica; edited a newspaper; and advocated pride in the blackness of the pure Negro. It has been suggested that Love's racial preachings inspired a young Jamaican, Marcus Garvey. Holly to Langford, May 14,

1889, Haiti Papers; Foreign Committee Minutes, November 9, 1887; Padgett, "Diplomats to Haiti and Their Diplomacy," p. 296; Alexander Crummell to John E. Bruce, January 17, 1884; April 25, 1893; May 21, 1896; July 30, 1897; March 5, 1898, Bruce Papers, Schomburg Collection; Robert A. Hill to David Dean, September 9, 1971.
19
Holly to Kimber, November 7, 1884, Haiti Papers.
20
Holly to Lee, February 21, 1882; to Kimber, October 16, 1883, Haiti Papers; Spenser St. John, *Hayti; or the Black Republic* (London: Smith, Elder and Co., 1883), p. 136.
21
Foreign Committee Minutes, February 2, November 12, 1877.
22
Holly to William H. Whittingham, June 21, 1877, Maryland Diocesan Archives; Holly to Kimber, December 6, 10, 1877, Haiti Papers.
23
Foreign Committee Minutes, June 8, 1880; Lee to Kimber, in Foreign Committee Minutes, September 14, 1880.
24
Charles B. Hall, "Mexico, Haiti and the Constitution," *A. M. E. Church Review* XLIX (April 1887): 338–351; *Churchman,* Supplement, November 3, 1883; *Journal of the General Convention* (1883): 90; William F. Brand, *Life of William Rollinson Whittingham, Fourth Bishop of Maryland* 2 vols. (New York: E. & J. B. Young, 1886), I: 248–278.
25
Holly to Kimber, November 22, December 10, 1883, Haiti Papers; Kimber to Holly, December 19, 1883, Foreign Committee Correspondence Sent.
26
Hall, "Mexico, Haiti and the Constitution," pp. 337–338.
27
The *Advance* (October 1887).
28
Holly to Kimber, March 1, April 5, May 27, June 13, 27, 1884; to James Brown, May 1, 1884, Haiti Papers; E. Walter Roberts to Holly, May 19, 1884; Kimber to Holly, May 20, June 17, 1884, Foreign Committee Correspondence Sent.

## IX    Defender of the Race

1
Holly to Alfred Lee, February 21, 1882, Haiti Papers; Holly, *God and the Negro,* p. 14; Holly to William McClain, June 25, 1850, American Colonization Society Papers.
2
Holly to Richard Duane, June 9, 1873, Haiti Papers; Ebenezer Bassett to Frederick Douglass, August 18, 1889, Frederick Douglass Papers; St. John, *Hayti, or the Black Republic,* pp. vi–ix.
3
St. John, *Hayti,* pp. ix, 22, 118, 131, 132, 143, 163.
4
London *Guardian,* Supplement, February 18, 1885.
5
Holly to Joshua Kimber, March 19, 1885, Haiti Papers; Philadelphia *Times,* June 6, 1893.
6
Holly to Kimber, March 19, 1885, Haiti Papers; London *Guardian,* Supplement, February 18, 1885.
7
Alonzo P. B. Holly to the editor, New York *Freeman,* August 26, 1886; Theodore Faustin Holly to the editor, ibid., September 15, 1886; New York *Age,* January 8, 1887.
8
Leyburn, *The Haitian People,* pp. 132, 334.
9
Holly, *Annual Report,* July 3, 1879, Haiti Papers; Holly, *First Semi-Annual Statement of Bishop of Haiti in Regard to Haiti Education Fund,* May 25, 1876, Lambeth Library Archives.

10

Ibid.; Holly to Samuel Denison, April 13, 1867; March 8, 1876; to William Langford, September 24, 1888, Haiti Papers.

11

Holly to Denison, April 13, 1867; to Duane, May 10, 1875; to Kimber, October 16, 1883, Haiti Papers; Holly, *Annual Report*, March 14, 1874, Haiti Papers; Leyburn, *The Haitian People*, pp. 93–101. See also Rotberg with Clague, *Haiti: The Politics of Squalor.*

12

Holly to Kimber, June 26, 1881, Haiti Papers; John Payne to Denison, August 12, 1869, Liberia Papers; Hollis R. Lynch, *Edward Wilmot Blyden, Pan Negro Patriot* (London: Oxford University Press, 1967), pp. 105–139. Crummell and Blyden worked to undermine the mulatto leadership in Liberia. In 1882 Blyden as president of Liberia College awarded the honorary degree of Doctor of Laws to "His Lordship, James T. Holly, Bishop of Haiti and an ardent lover to his race." Blyden to William Coppinger, January 20, 1882, American Colonization Society Papers.

13

Holly to Kimber, March 4, May 2, June 3, 1902, Haiti Papers.

14

Holly to Duane, March 17, 1876, Haiti Papers. Holly applied the epithet "foreign adventurer" indiscriminately to either European or American diplomats or businessmen and to members of the mulatto elite of Haiti. Holly to John W. Wood, February 14, 1898, Haiti Papers.

15

Holly to Langford, March 7, 1889; April 8, 1891, Haiti Papers; Holly to Virginia Protestants, June 1889, in George F. Bragg, Jr., *First Churchman on Southern Soil* (Baltimore: Church Advocate Press, 1907), p. 63.

16

*Church Advocate,* July 1907; Holly to Virginia Protestants, June 1899, in Bragg, *First Churchman on Southern Soil,* p. 63.

17

"If Diogenes had walked about the streets of the United States with his lighted candle at mid-day looking for an honest man, he would have him ... in Grover Cleveland." Holly to Langford, June 29, 1893, Haiti Papers. See also Holly to Kimber, May 13, 1898, Haiti Papers.

18

Langston, *Plantation to Capitol,* pp. 360–362, 373–374, 397–400.

19

Holly to the editor, New York *Age,* March 26, 1887. The editorial appeared in the same issue. For a fuller description of the Lazare and Pelletier claims, see Ludwell Montague, *Haiti and the United States, 1714–1938,* 1940, reprint (New York: Russell and Russell, 1966), pp. 115–123; and Rayford W. Logan, *The Diplomatic Relations of the United States with Haiti, 1779–1891* (Chapel Hill: University of North Carolina Press, 1940), pp. 310–311.

20

Langston, *Plantation to Capitol,* pp. 394–395; St. John, *Hayti,* p. 241; New York *Age,* March 26, 1887; Holly to Langford, May 13, 1888, Haiti Papers; H. C. C. Astwood to the editor, New York *Age,* April 2, 1887; Holly to Douglass, December 20, 1893, Frederick Douglass Papers.

21

Philip Foner, *Frederick Douglass* (New York: Citadel Press, 1964), pp. 355–367; Montague, *Haiti and the United States,* p. 162; Holly to Langford, November 2, 1894; March 25, 1896, Haiti Papers; Holly to Douglass, December 20, 1893; Alexandre Battiste to Douglass, August 1, September 24, 1891, Frederick Douglass Papers.

22

Holly to Langford, December 1, 1886, April 8, 1891; to Kimber, July 31, November 6, 1902, Haiti Papers; James Theodore Holly, "Spread Eagleism," *A. M. E. Church Review* XVI (January 1900): 338. Although Holly disliked all capitalistic exploiters, "whether they be clothed in a black, yellow or white skin," he seemed to take a certain pride in admitting to T. Thomas Fortune that Haiti possessed some of the most adept "black adventurers" in the New World. New York *Freeman,* April 25, 1885.

23

Holly to Kimber, November 6, 1902, Haiti Papers. See also August Meier, *Negro Thought in America, 1880–1915* (Ann Arbor: University of Michigan Press, 1963), pp. 46–47.

24
James Theodore Holly, "Socialism from the Biblical Point of View," *A. M. E. Church Review* IX (December 1892): 244-258.
25
Holly's favorite economist was the French utopian socialist, Charles Fourier, "the most Christ-hearted man that has trodden our planet since the days of Jesus and his apostles," ibid., p. 254; James Theodore Holly, "Bi-metallism and Industrialism," *A. M. E. Church Review* XIV (July 1897): 146-155; Holly to Langford, April 8, 1891, Haiti Papers.
26
Holly, "Socialism from a Biblical Point of View," pp. 244-258.
27
Holly to Kimber, May 10, 1875, Haiti Papers; Holly to Canon Fulcher, March 10, 1894, Bishops Biographical File, Church Historical Society; James Theodore Holly, "Political Economy," *A. M. E. Church Review* X (October 1893): 218-219. Only a tiny minority of Episcopalians espoused millenarianism in the late nineteenth century. Among the more notable was Stephen H. Tyng, one of Holly's patrons in the early 1860s. In 1873 many millenarians participated in the founding of the Reformed Episcopal Church. See Paul Carter, "The Reformed Episcopal Schism of the Protestant Episcopal Church," *Historical Magazine of the Protestant Episcopal Church* XXXIII (September 1964): 225-238; and Ernest Sandeen, *The Roots of Fundamentalism, British and American Millenarianism. 1800-1930* (Chicago: University of Chicago Press, 1970).
28
Holly, "Socialism from a Biblical Point of View," p. 258; James Theodore Holly, "Sacred Chronology and Arithmetic of Divine Revelation," *A. M. E. Church Review* VI (July 1885): 9-12; Holly "Spread Eagleism," p. 339; Holly to Kimber, March 4, 1902, Haiti Papers.
29
James Theodore Holly, "The Origins of Race Antagonism," *Arena* XXI (April 1899): 422-426.
30
Sermon of James Theodore Holly, July 25, 1878, printed in Holly, *God and the Negro,* pp. 149-150.

# X     The Bishop of Haiti

1
Holly to George Flichtner, March 8, 1882, Haiti Papers; Holly, *Annual Report,* July 2, 1900, Haiti Papers; St. John, *Hayti,* p. 255.
2
Holly to William Hare, March 5, 1872; to Joshua Kimber, July 3, 1881, Haiti Papers.
3
Holly to William Langford, March 20, 23, 1886, Haiti Papers.
4
Holly to Kimber, May 27, June 14, 1884; April 23, 1903; to John W. Wood, July 22, 1903, Haiti Papers.
5
St. Denis Bauduy to Hare, April 20, 1872; Charles E. Benedict to Kimber, September 10, 1883; Holly to Langford, March 18, 1889; Pierre E. Jones to Kimber, May 8, 1908; memorandum of Jones interview with Wood, March 24, 1911, Haiti Papers.
6
See Holly's *Annual Reports* to the board of Missions for yearly baptismal and confirmation statistics. This imbalance in statistics did not end with Holly's episcopate. In 1955, the Missionary District of Haiti reported 57,158 baptized members and less that 10,000 confirmed communicants. See Joseph G. Moore, "A Study of the Episcopal Church in the Missionary District of Haiti" (unpublished report, The Unit of Research and Field Study of the National Council of the Protestant Episcopal Church, 1956), pp. 48-49.
7
Holly to Langford, March 14, 1885, Haiti Papers; "The Republic of Haiti," in *Handbooks on the Missions of the Episcopal Church* V (New York: National Council of the Protestant Episcopal Church, 1926), p. 36.

8
Holly to William Bacon Stevens, October 21, 1876, Southard Hay Collection, Sterling Library, Yale University; Holly, "Circular Letter to American Churchmen," July 15, 1882, Haiti Papers; Holly to Flichtner, March 8, 1882; to Kimber, February 16, 1883; March 6, 1885; December 30, 1890; July 20, 1897; January 30, March 17, 1904, Haiti Papers; *Pacific Churchman,* December 15, 1901. Among Holly's unrealized hopes were two additional farm schools to serve the people north and south of Haiti.
9
Holly, *Annual Report,* July 8, 1882; July 1905, Haiti Papers; Holly to Wood, February 15, 1900; to Kimber, December 21, 1901, Haiti Papers.
10
Holly, *Annual Report,* July 4, 1894, Haiti Papers; Holly to Kimber, March 13, 1885; to Langford, April 13, 1889; Kimber to Holly, December 27, 1895, quoted by Holly to Langford, February 1, 1896, Haiti Papers; Langford to Holly, May 20, June 18, 1889, Foreign Committee Correspondence Sent; "The Republic of Haiti," in *Handbooks on the Missions of the Episcopal Church* V, 2.
11
Holly to Langford, July 7, 1888; August 25, 1891; November 23, 1893; November 24, 1894; March 13, 1895; to Kimber, January 7, 1890, Haiti Papers; Langford to Holly, August 3, 1888; May 26, 1893; George Bliss to Holly, September 13, 1895; Kimber to Holly, December 1, 1905, Foreign Committee Correspondence Sent.
12
Holly to Langford, September 19, 1895; August 13, November 26, 1896; June 25, 1897, Haiti Papers; Holly, *Annual Report,* July 1897, Haiti Papers.
13
Holly to Kimber, November 9, 1888, Haiti Papers.
14
Holly to Richard Duane, October 9, 1873; to Kimber, November 9, 1888. Very few personal details about Sarah Henly Holly are found in her husband's correspondence. Her intelligence may be presumed from the success of her children, and it is obvious that she shared James's hopes and aspirations for them. Active in church work, she headed the women's auxiliary of Holy Trinity Church for many years.
15
Circular letter of James Theodore Holly to the American bishops, noted in Holly to Langford, January 14, 1888; Holly to Kimber, March 13, 18, April 7, 1889, Haiti Papers; Holly, *Annual Report,* July 4, 1884, Haiti Papers.
16
Holly to Langford, October 27, 1887; March 18, 1889; June 15, 1892; to Arthur S. Lloyd, September 13, 1904, Haiti Papers; Holly to Mrs. George Burgess, August 18, 1894, Connecticut Diocesan Archives.
17
Holly, *Annual Report,* July 1, 1898, Haiti Papers; Holly to Langford, March 7, November 29, 1894; to Kimber, January 19, 1884; November 19, 1901; to Lloyd, September 13, 1904, Haiti Papers; Nancy Gordon Heinl, "First Black Episcopal Bishop," North American Newspaper Alliance press release, November 8, 1974. Holly was always sensitive about his lack of transportation. In 1884 he had written that the Wesleyan superintendent enjoyed his own horse and buggy while "the Bishop of Haiti makes his Port-au-Prince rounds on his apostolic shanks," Holly to Kimber, January 19, 1884, Haiti Papers.

# XI    The Final Thrust

1
"The Bishop of Haiti," *Quarterly Message Concerning Church Missions,* VI, p. 36; Holly to Joshua Kimber, July 9, 1908, Haiti Papers.
2
Holly to the editor, *Voice of the Fugitive,* May 7, 1851; James Theodore Holly, "West Indies Confederacy for the Negro," New York *Journal,* February 2, 1902.
3
Holly to Alexander Crummell, April 22, 1864, Alexander Crummell Papers, Schomburg Collection; Holly to Kimber, March 10, 1909, Haiti Papers; Holly, "West Indies Confederacy for the Negro."

4

Lynch, *Edward Wilmot Blyden,* p. 107; New York *Age,* January 7, 1889. See also Edwin Redkey, *Black Exodus: Black Nationalist and Back to Africa Movements, 1890–1910* (New Haven: Yale University Press, 1969); and Cyril Griffith, *The African Dream: Martin R. Delany and the Emergence of Pan-African Thought* (University Park: The Pennsylvania State University Press, 1975).

5

Holly to Mary E. Bibb Cary, August 6, 1862, in *Pine and Palm,* September 6, 1862; Holly to Kimber, April 2, 1902, Haiti Papers; Holly, "West Indies Confederacy for the Negro," New York *Journal,* February 2, 1902.

6

Holly to Kimber, June 12, 1899, Haiti Papers; George Padmore, ed., *History of the Pan African Conference* (London: Hammersmith Bookshop, 1963), pp. 3–9; Immanuel Geiss, "Notes on the Development of Pan-Afrikanism," *Journal of the Historical Society of Nigeria* III (June 1967): 719–725. See also Geiss, *Pan Afrikanismus* (Frankfurt-am-Main: Europaische Verlagsanstätt, 1968); and Owen C. Mathurin, *Henry Sylvester Williams and the Origins of the Pan-African Movement, 1869–1911* (Westport: Greenwood Press, 1976).

7

Geiss, "Notes on the Development of Pan-Afrikanism"; London *Times,* July 26, 1900. See also Alexander Walters, *My Life and My Work* (New York: R. H. Revell Co., 1917), pp. 253–264; and James R. Hooker, *Henry Sylvester Williams: Imperial Pan-Africanist* (London: Collings, 1975), pp. 28–38.

8

Holly to Kimber, May 2, 1902, Haiti Papers; Holly, West Indies Confederacy for the Negro."

9

James Van Buren to John W. Wood, February 24, 1905; Arthur R. Gray to Charles Colmore, May 1, 1917; Domestic and Foreign Missionary Society Papers: Puerto Rico, Archives and Historical Collections—Episcopal Church. The statements in the paragraph are based upon an examination of the yearly *Proceedings of the Board of Managers of the Domestic and Foreign Missionary Society.*

10

James Theodore Holly, "A Christmas Plea," December 1900, Haiti Papers. For the fiscal year 1899–1900 Haiti received approximately $7,000 from the American church and listed 554 communicants and 13 ordained missionaries. Liberia received $57,000 and listed 1,633 communicants and 18 ordained missionaries. China received $69,000 and listed 1,180 communicants and 46 ordained missionaries. Japan received $89,000 and listed 2,357 communicants and 46 ordained missionaries. A missionary bishop had been in residence in each of these countries for several years before Holly was consecrated for Haiti.

11

Holly to Wood, April 2, 1902, Haiti Papers; *Churchman,* October 26, 1901.

12

Holly to Kimber, April 16, October 16, 1901; March 10, 1902, Haiti Papers; *Journal of the General Convention* (1902): 21.

13

Holly to Kimber, January 2, 1902; to Lloyd, January 21, 1902; Haiti Papers; "Report of the Bishop of Haiti," *Proceedings of the Board of Managers,* 1902, p. 219. The aging Joshua Kimber had given over all his decision-making power to Lloyd and Wood.

14

Holly to Kimber, June 4, 1903; January 30, 1904; January 13, April 27, 1905; to Lloyd, March 9, 1903; to Wood, September 22, 1904, Haiti Papers.

15

Kimber to Holly, March 1, 1905, Foreign Committee Correspondence Sent. Most white Episcopalians wanted any Negro who might become a bishop to serve as a suffragan or assistant to a white diocesan bishop. Black Episcopalians demanded independent Negro missionary bishops to serve an independent Negro Episcopal church. A vocal white supporter of the Negro position was William M. Brown, Bishop of Arkansas. He argued that separation of Afro-American and Anglo-American churchmen was necessary "to save them from mutual degradation." Those white critics who opposed a Negro episcopate because of a belief in the moral and intellectual deficiencies of the black man, he said, only had to examine the career of James Theodore Holly for an example of a Negro doing "excellent work with the materials and facilities at hand." William M. Brown, *The Crucial Race Question* (Little Rock: Arkansas Churchman, 1907), pp. ix, x, xxx, 55–56, 244; *Church Advocate,* October 1907.

16
A lack of communication, if not estrangement, between American churchmen and Holly was apparent as early as 1903. At that time the missionary bishop of Puerto Rico wrote to Lloyd "that I have received the impression that our relations with Bishop Holly are such as to render it doubtful that we can expand our work into the areas of San Domingo not under the Republic of Haiti." Five years later the missionary bishop of Cuba, whose vessel was anchored in the harbor of Port-au-Prince, failed to come ashore to visit Holly. Van Buren to Lloyd, September 3, 1903, Puerto Rico Papers; Pierre E. Jones to Kimber, February 5, 1908, Haiti Papers; Kimber to Holly, February 21, 1908, Foreign Committee Correspondence Sent.
17
Holly to Lloyd, July 6, 1908; to Kimber, July 9, 1908; clipping from Le Nouvelliste (Port-au-Prince), July 8, 1908, Haiti Papers; Church Advocate, December 1908.
18
Memo of John W. Wood, December 10, 1908; Holly to Kimber, December 31, 1908, Haiti Papers.
19
Arthur C. Holly to O. W. Whittaker, February 13, 1910; James Theodore Holly to Kimber, May 29, 1908; to Wood, September 10, 1909; clipping from Le Nouvelliste, September 14, 1909, Haiti Papers.
20
Lloyd to Holly, April 27, 1909, Foreign Committee Correspondence Sent; translation of article in Le Nouvelliste, October 4, 1909; Holly to Kimber, November 11, 1909; Wood, memorandum of interview with Pierre E. Jones, March 24, 1911, Haiti Papers; Church Advocate, December 1909.
21
Minutes of the Board of Managers, March 8, 1910; Arthur C. Holly to Whittaker, March 13, 1910, Haiti Papers.
22
Grace Theodora Holly to Anna Paige, March 1911, in Church Advocate, June 1911; John Alfred Holly to Wood, March 4, 23, 1911, Haiti Papers.
23
Charles E. Benedict to Kimber, March 18, 1911, Haiti Papers; Grace Theodora Holly to Paige, March 1911, in Church Advocate, June 1911.
24
Church Advocate, June 1911.
25
Spirit of Missions LXXI (April 1911): 284; Minutes of the Board of Managers, May 3, 1911; Kimber to Arthur C. Holly; to Alonzo P. Holly, April 3, 1911, Foreign Committee Correspondence Sent.

## Epilogue

1
Holly's personality traits are ones that he also admired in other black leaders. See his eulogy of Martin R. Delany, "In Memoriam," A. M. E. Church Review III (October 1886) 117–125.

2
"The Republic of Haiti," Handbooks on the Missions of the Episcopal Church, V, p. 34. What happened subsequently to Holly's beloved Orthodox Apostolic Church of Haiti? Differences of opinion concerning its proper role in the future existed among his followers, including his own sons, at the time of his death. Barely a week afterward, Arthur C. Holly wrote to Joshua Kimber that "the movement is ripe not only to replace him but also to realize a generous reform and especially such as will give to the mother mission a greater scope of action." The next year the convocation of the Haiti church petitioned the board of managers to abolish their covenant with the Orthodox Apostolic Church and constitute Haiti a regular missionary district of the American church. This was done, and a series of "Bishops in Charge" was followed by two white missionary bishops of Haiti, Harry R. Carson and C. Alfred Voegeli, who served successively from 1923 to 1970. In April 1971 Luc Garnier, a native of Haiti, was consecrated bishop. The country still remains a missionary district of the American church. Arthur C. Holly to Kimber, February 3, March 23, 1911; Sabourin Holly to the board of managers, September 27, 1911; pastoral letter to the members of the Orthodox Apostolic Church in Haiti, ca.

June 1912, Haiti Papers; *Journal of the General Convention* (1913): 38; H. R. Carson, *A First Survey of Haiti* (New York: National Council, ca. 1924).

3

The current bishop of Haiti, Luc Garnier, in speaking of Holly's "historical significance" to the church in Haiti, has remarked: "through his strength, convictions and vast courage he introduced and developed his religion to persons mainly unreceptive, in an unfamiliar climate and language. That he succeeded valiantly speaks for itself," Luc Garnier to David Dean, June 17, 1971. In February 1975 the National Cathedral in Washington and the Black Episcopal Clergy Association in the District of Columbia sponsored "A Commemoration of the Centennial of the Consecration of James Theodore Holly as first Bishop of Haiti and first Afro-American Episcopal Bishop."

4

Holly, "Thoughts on Hayti," p. 365.

# Bibliography

I. Manuscripts

A

In the Archives and Historical Collections—Episcopal Church (formerly the Church Historical Society), Austin, Texas. The Archives is the official depository of the Archives of the General Convention of the Protestant Episcopal Church in the United States.

Bishop's Biographical File.
    This collection contains about a dozen relevant items, 1886–1936, including Holly letters and three photographs of the bishop.

Domestic and Foreign Missionary Society: China Papers, 1850–1911.

Domestic and Foreign Missionary Society: Foreign Committee Correspondence Sent, 1855–1911.
    These letterbooks contain copies of the numerous letters sent to Holly by missionary officials in the Church Missions House.

Domestic and Foreign Missionary Society: Haiti Papers, 1855–1939.
    This collection is the most important source of information for a biography of James Theodore Holly. The papers contain over 4,000 letters, including nearly 1,100 of Holly's to various church officials in the United States. While many of these letters are reprinted in the official organ of the Domestic and Foreign Missionary Society, the *Spirit of Missions,* a researcher should be aware that many missionary letters, from all fields, were heavily edited by the foreign secretary and expunged of nearly all critical remarks.

Domestic and Foreign Missionary Society: Liberia Papers, 1850–1890.

Domestic and Foreign Missionary Society: Minutes of the Board of Managers, 1877–1911.

Domestic and Foreign Missionary Society: Minutes of the Foreign Committee, 1850–1880.

Domestic and Foreign Missionary Society: Personnel Files, 1835–1911.

Domestic and Foreign Missionary Society: Puerto Rico Papers, 1900–1920.

Minutes of the Executive Committee of the American Church Missionary Society, 1862–1865.

Proceedings of the American Church Missionary Society, 1860–1872.

Thomas Collection of Bishops' Autographs, 1884 and 1905.
    There are two Holly letters in this collection.

B
In the National Archives.

U.S. Department of Commerce. Bureau of the Census. Eighth Census of the United States: 1860. Manuscript returns of Schedule I, Free Inhabitants for New Haven, Connecticut.

U.S. Department of Commerce. Bureau of the Census. Seventh Census of the United States: 1850. Manuscript returns of Schedule I, Free Inhabitants for Burlington, Vermont.

U.S. Department of State. Consular Despatches, Port-au-Prince, Haiti, 1835–1906.

U.S. Department of State. Diplomatic Despatches, Haiti, 1862–1906.

C
Other Manuscript Collections.

American Colonization Society Papers, Library of Congress, Washington, D.C., 1849–1880.
    This collection contains a half dozen relevant items, including three Holly letters.

American Missionary Association Papers, Fisk University, Nashville, Tennessee.
    This collection contains one Holly letter for 1862.

Amos G. Beman Scrapbooks, Beinecke Rare Book and Manuscript Library, Yale University, New Haven, Connecticut.

Archbishop of Canterbury Papers, Lambeth Library, London.
This collection contains a half dozen Holly letters, 1869–1880.

Bishops Papers, Connecticut Diocesan Archives, Trinity Library, Hartford, Connecticut.
This collection contains about a dozen Holly letters, 1875–1902.

Bishops Papers, Maryland Diocesan Archives, Maryland Historical Society, Annapolis, Maryland.
This collection contains six Holly items, 1874–1878.

Bishops Papers, Pierpont Morgan Library, New York City.
This collection contains three Holly letters, 1873–1888.

John E. Bruce Papers, Schomburg Collection, Harlem Branch, New York Public Library.
This collection contains one Holly letter from 1891 and several Alexander Crummell letters from the 1890s.

Alexander Crummell Papers, Schomburg Collection, Harlem Branch, New York Public Library.
This collection contains one Holly letter from 1864.

Frederick Douglass Papers, Library of Congress, Washington, D.C.
This collection contains one Holly letter from 1893 and several letters of Ebenezer Bassett and Alexandre Battiste that mention Holly.

Haiti Collection of Manuscripts, Rare Books Room, Boston Public Library.

Southard Hay Collection, Sterling Library, Yale University, New Haven, Connecticut,
This collection contains several Holly items, 1875–1877.

Leonidas Polk Papers, Sterling Library, Yale University, New Haven, Connecticut.
This collection contains one Holly letter from 1860.

Protestant Episcopal Bishops Collection, Sterling Library, Yale University, New Haven, Connecticut.
This collection contains two Holly letters, 1875–1878.

James Redpath Letterbook, Library of Congress, Washington, D.C.
This letterbook details Redpath's work with the Haytian Emigration Bureau between March 30 and December 27, 1861.

James Redpath Letterbook, Schomburg Collection, New York Public Library.
This letterbook details Redpath's work with the Haytian Emigration Bureau
between December 31, 1861, and May 12, 1862.

St Luke's Church, New Haven, Connecticut. Minutes of Meetings, Financial
Statements, 1844–1896.
These are housed in St. Luke's Church and are indispensable for any discus-
sion of Holly's church work in New Haven.

St. Luke's Church, New Haven, Connecticut. Parish Records, Financial Statements, 1845–1885.
These are housed in St. Luke's Church and are indispensable for any discussion of Holly's church work in New Haven.

Lewis Tappan Papers, Library of Congress, Washington, D.C.
This collection contains two letters from Tappan to Holly, dated 1864.

United Society for the Propagation of the Gospel, London.
This collection contains a half dozen Holly items, 1874–1880.

II. Newspapers and Magazines

A
Negro Newspapers and Magazines, United States and Canada.

*A. M. E. Church Review* (Philadelphia), 1884–1911.
*Anglo-African* (New York), 1859–1865.
*Anglo-African Magazine* (New York), 1859–1860.
*Church Advocate* (Baltimore), 1907–1921.
*Douglass Monthly* (Rochester), 1858–1863.
*Frederick Douglass' Paper* (Rochester), 1851–1857.
*New National Era* (Washington), 1871.
New York *Age,* 1887–1911.
New York *Freeman,* 1884–1887.
*North Star* (Rochester), 1847–1851.
*People's Advocate* )Alexandria, Va.), 1878–1879.
*Provincial Freeman* (Windsor, Toronto), 1853–1858.
*Voice of the Fugitive* (Sandwich, Windsor), 1851–1853.

B
Haitian Newspapers.

*Le Bien Public,* March 23, 1866.

*Le Peuple,* July 13, 1874.
*Le Nouvelliste,* July 7, 1888; October 4, 1909.

C

White Newspapers and Magazines, American and English.

*The Advance* (Baltimore), 1887.
*African Repository* (Washington), 1845–1892.
*American Freemason* (Louisville, New York). 1858–1860.
*Ashlar* (Chicago, Detroit), 1855–1861.
Burlington *Free Press,* 1849–1855.
*Calendar* (Hartford, Conn.), 1855–1866.
*Church Journal* (New York), 1853–1878.
*Church Times* (London), 1878.
*Churchman* (Hartford), 1866–1911.
*Liberator* (Boston), 1848–1865.
*Living Church* (Milwaukee), 1925.
London *Guardian,* 1855.
London *Times,* 1878, 1899–1901.
*National Anti-Slavery Standard* (New York), 1850–1861.
New Haven *Daily Morning Journal and Courier,* 1861.
New York *Journal,* 1902.
New York *Sun,* 1896.
*New York Times,* 1911.
*Niles' Weekly Register* (Philadelphia), 1818–1825.
*Pacific Churchman* (San Francisco), 1900–1912.
Philadelphia *Times,* 1893.
*Pine and Palm* (Boston, New York), 1861–1862.
*Spirit of Missions* (New York), 1850–1925.

III. Journals, Reports, Proceedings

American Church Missionary Society. *Reports,* 1860–1872.

Anglo Continental Society. *Reports,* 1865–1875.

Domestic and Foreign Missionary Society. *Proceedings of Missionary Council of
    the Board of Managers, Reports of Bishops . . .etc.,* 1850–1913.

General Convention of the Protestant Episcopal Church in the United States of
    America. *Journal,* 1853–1925.

Maryland Colonization Society. *Journal,* 1850–1861.

New York Colonization Society. *Journal,* 1850–1863.

Protestant Episcopal Church. Diocese of Connecticut. *Journal,* 1854–1867.

Protestant Episcopal Church. Diocese of Michigan. *Journal,* 1852–1861.

IV.\ U.S. Government Publications

"Foreign Relations: Hayti," *House Executive Document* 1873, 45 Cong., 2 Sess. I, No. 1, Part 1.

"Special Report of the Commissioner of Education on the Condition and Improvement of Public Schools in the District of Columbia," *House Executive Document* 315, 41 Cong., 2 Sess., Vol. 13, Serial 1427.

U.S. Bureau of the Census. *Negro Population, 1790–1815.* Washington, D.C., 1918.

U.S. Census Office. *Heads of Families at the First Census of the United States Taken in the Year 1790.* Washington, D.C., 1907.

V. Published Writings of James Theodore Holly,
A Select List

A
Pamphlets and Books.

*A Christmas Plea.* New York, 1900.

*The Establishment of the Church in Haiti.* New Haven, 1860.

*Facts About the Church Mission in Haiti.* New York, 1896.

*The Form of Ordaining or Consecrating a Bishop Used at Grace Church, New York, on the Twenty-third Sunday after Trinity, Nov. 8, 1874, on Occasion of the Consecration of the Rev. James Theodore Holly, D.D., Dean of the Convocation of Haiti and Bishop-Elect of the Protestant Episcopal Church on the Island of Haiti.* New York, 1874.

*Manuel do Théologie Dogmatique ou Résume des Chefs de la Science Sacrée à l'Usage du Clergé De l'Eglise Orthodoxe Apostolique en Haiti.* Port-au-Prince, 1879.

*Vindication of the Capacity of the Negro Race for Self Government and Civilized Progress.* New Haven, 1857.

*The Word of God, against ecclesiastical imperialism set forth in a letter addressed to Bishop Daniel A. Payne, the senior bishop of the AME Church by the Rt. Rev. James Theodore Holly, Bishop of Haiti.* New York, n.d.

**B**
Articles.

"Biblical Criticism," *A. M. E. Church Review* IV (1887): 365–368.

"Biblical Inspiration," *A. M. E. Church Review* XII (1895):181–190.

"Bimetallism and Industrialism," *A. M. E. Church Review* XIV (1897): 146–155.

"Christian Missions in Haiti," *Missionary Review of the World* XXVI (1903): 645–653.

"The Ethnological Development of the Divine Plan of Human Redemption," *A. M. E. Church Review* I (1884): 79–85.

"The Higher Criticism," *A. M. E. Church Review* XI (1895): 329–335.

"In Memoriam," *A. M. E. Church Review* III (1886): 117–125.

"Musings on the Kingdom of Christ," *Anglo-African Magazine* II (1860): 45–48, 65–68.

"The Number of the Beast, 666," *American Church Review* XXXI (1879): 285–291.

"The Origins of Race Antagonisms," *Arena* XXI (1889): 421–426.

"The Philosophy of Language," *A. M. E. Church Review* XIII (1896): 102–112.

"Political Economy," *A. M. E. Church Review* X (1893): 213–219.

"Sacred Chronology and Arithmetic of Divine Revelation," *A. M. E. Church Review* II (1885): 9–15.

"Socialism from the Biblical Point of View," *A. M. E. Church Review* IX (1892): 244–259.

"Spread-Eagleism," *A. M. E. Church Review* XVI (1900): 332–339.

"Thoughts on Hayti," *Anglo-African Magazine* I (1859): 185–187, 219–221, 241–243, 298–300, 327–329, 363–367; II (1860): 15–18.

"Tribute to Bishop Burns of Liberia," *African Repository* XXXIX (1863): 324–331.

"West Indies Confederacy for the Negro," New York *Journal,* February 2, 1902.

VI. Books and Pamphlets

Addison, James Thayer. *The Episcopal Church in the United States.* New York, 1951.

Bassett, Ebenezer. *Handbook of Haiti.* Washington, D.C., 1893.

Batterson, Herman G. *A Sketchbook of the American Episcopate.* Philadelphia, 1884.

Bedell, Gregory T. *The Canterbury Pilgrimage, To and From the Lambeth Conference and Sheffield Congress.* New York, 1878.

Bibb, Henry. *Narrative of the Life and Adventures of Henry Bibb, an American Slave.* New York, 1850.

Bird, Mark Baker. *The Black Man, or Haytian Independence.* New York, 1869.

Blair, Francis Preston, Jr. *The Destiny of the Races of this Continent. An address delivered before the Mercantile Library Association of Boston, Massachusetts, on the 26th of January 1859. With Appendix.* Washington, D.C., 1859.

———— *Speech of Hon. Frank P. Blair, Jr., of Missouri, on the acquisition of territory in Central and South America, to be colonized with free blacks, and held as a dependency by the United States, on the 14th day of January, 1858. With an Appendix.* Washington, D.C., 1858.

Board of Education of New Haven City School District. *Annual Report.* New Haven, 1856.

———— *Manual, 1856-1857.* New Haven, 1857.

Bragg, George F., Jr. *The First Negro Priest on Southern Soil.* Baltimore, 1907.

———— *History of the Afro-American Group of the Episcopal Church.* Baltimore, 1922.

———— *Men of Maryland.* Baltimore, 1914.

Brand, William F. *Life of William Rollinson Wittingham, Fourth Bishop of Maryland.* New York, 1886.

Brown, William M. *The Crucial Race Question.* Little Rock, 1907.

Brown, William Wells. *The Black Man, his antecedents, his genius and his achievements.* New York, 1863.

Buffalo. *Commercial Directory for the City of Buffalo,* 1855.

Burgess, Alexander, ed. *Memoir of the Life of the Right Reverend George Burgess, D.D.* Philadelphia, 1869.

Burgess, George. *Last Journal of the Rt. Rev. George Burgess, D.D.* Boston, 1866.

Carlisle, Rodney P. *The Roots of Black Nationalism.* Port Washington, 1975.

Carson, Harry R. *A First Survey of Haiti.* New York, ca. 1924.

Colored National Convention. *Proceedings of the Colored National Convention.* Rochester, 1853.

Cooke, Jacob E. *Frederick Bancroft, Historian.* Norman, 1957.

Cromwell, John W. *The Negro in American History, Men and Women Eminent in the Evolution of the American of African Descent.* Washington, D.C., 1914.

Curtis, William R. *The Lambeth Conferences, the Solution for Pan-Anglican Organization.* New York, 1942.

D'Alaux, Gustave. *Soulouque and His Empire.* Richmond, 1861.

Davis, H. P. *Black Democracy, the Story of Haiti.* New York, 1967, ca. 1928.

Delany, Martin R. *The Condition, Elevation, Emigration and Destiny of Colored People of the United States.* Philadelphia, 1852.

———. *Blake or the Huts of Africa.* Edited by Floyd T. Miller. Boston, 1970.

———. "Official Report of the Niger Valley Exploring Party." Reprinted in Howard H. Bell, ed., *Search for a Plane.* Ann Arbor, 1970.

DeMille, George E. *The Catholic Movement in the American Episcopal Church.* Philadelphia, 1941.

[Dewey, Loring]. *Correspondence Relative to the Emigration to Hayti, of the Free People of Colour in the United States.* New York, 1824.

Douglass, Frederick; W. T. Watkins; and T. M. Whitfield. *Arguments, Pro and Con on the Call for a National Emigration Convention to be held at Cleveland, Ohio, August 1854 with a short appendix of the statistics of Canada West, West Indies, Central and South America.* Detroit, 1854.

Dyer, Heman. *Records of an Active Life.* New York, 1900, ca. 1886.

Emery, Julia C. *A Century of Endeavours, 1821-1921, A Record of the First Hundred Years of the Missions of the Protestant Episcopal Church in the United States of America*. New York, 1921.

Foner, Philip S. *Frederick Douglass*. New York, 1964.

Geiss, Immanuel. *Pan Afrikanismus, Zur Geschichte der De Kolonisation*. Frankfurt-am-Main, 1968.

General Convention for the Improvement of the Colored Inhabitants of Canada. *Minutes and Proceedings of the General Convention for the Improvement of the Colored Inhabitants of Canada. Held by Adjournments in Amherstburgh C[anada] W[est], June 16th and 17th, 1853*. Windsor, 1853.

Gilman, Daniel Coit. *The Launching of a University and Other Papers*. New York, 1906.

Green, Constance M. *The Secret City, a History of Race Relations in the Nation's Capital*. Princeton, 1967.

Griffith, Cyril E. *The African Dream: Martin R. Delany and the Emergence of Pan-African Thought*. University Park, 1975.

Griffiths, Julia, ed. *Autographs for Freedom*. Rochester, 1854.

Grimshaw, William H. *Official History of Freemasonry Among the Colored People in North America*. New York, 1906.

Halliburton, Cecil D. *A History of St. Augustine's College, 1867-1937*. Raleigh, 1937.

Haytian Emigration Society. *Information for the free people of colour who are inclined to emigrate to Hayti*. New York, 1824.

Hazard, Samuel. *Santo Domingo past and present, with a glance at Haiti*. New York, 1873.

Hearne, William J., and Edwin V. Nostrand. *Brooklyn Alphabetical and Street Directory and Yearly Advertiser for 1844 and 1845*. Brooklyn, 1845.

Holly, Alonzo Potter. *The Problems of Our Race: Our Duties and Responsibilities*. Nassau, 1903.

————— *God and the Negro*. Nashville, 1937.

————— *Our Future Relations with Haiti*. Philadelphia, 1931.

Holly, Joseph C. *Freedom's Offerings.* Rochester, 1853.

Hooker, John R. *Henry Sylvester Williams.* London, 1975.

Katzman, David M. *Before the Ghetto: Black Detroit in the Nineteenth Century.* Urbana, 1973.

Knight, A. W. *Our Mission in Haiti.* New York, ca. 1923.

Langston, John Mercer. *From the Virginia Plantation to the National Capitol.* Hartford, 1894.

Leger, J. N. *Haiti, Her History and Her Detractors.* New York, 1907.

Leyburn, James G. *The Haitian People.* New York, 1941, rev. ed. 1966.

Litwack, Leon F. *North of Slavery: The Negro in the Free States, 1790-1860.* Chicago, 1961.

*Livre Bleu D'Haiti* [Blue Book of Haiti]. New York, 1919.

Logan, Rayford W. *The Diplomatic Relations of the United States with Haiti, 1776-1891.* Chapel Hill, 1941.

_____ *The Negro in American Life and Thought: The Nadir, 1877-1901.* New York, 1954.

Love, J. Robert. *Is Bishop Holly Innocent?* Port-au-Prince, 1883.

_____ *Proof of Bishop Holly's Guilt.* Port-Au-Prince, 1883.

Lynch, Hollis R. *Edward Wilmot Blyden, Pan-Negro Patriot.* London, 1967.

Mathurin, Owen C. *Henry Sylvester Williams and the Origins of the Pan-African Movement, 1869-1911.* Westport, 1976.

Meier, August. *Negro Thought in America, 1880-1915: Racial Ideologies in the Age of Booker T. Washington.* Ann Arbor, 1963.

Miller, Floyd John. *The Search for a Black Nationality: Black Emigration and Colonization, 1787-1863.* Urbana, 1975.

Montague, Ludwell Lee. *Haiti and the United States, 1714-1938.* New York, 1966, ca. 1940.

Munroe, William C. *A Brief History of St. Matthew's Protestant Episcopal Church.* Detroit (?), 1856 (?).

National Council of the Protestant Episcopal Church. *Handbooks on the Missions of the Episcopal Church.* New York, 1926.

Niles, Blair. *Black Haiti, A Biography of Africa's Eldest Daughter.* New York, 1926.

Orthodox Apostolic Church of Haiti. *Personal Letter. Port-au-Prince, 1911.*

Ott, Thomas O. *The Haitian Revolution, 1789-1804.* Knoxville, 1973.

Padmore, George, ed. *History of the Pan African Congress.* London, 1963, ca. 1947.

Pease, William H. and Jane H. *Black Utopia: Negro Communal Experiments in America.* Madison, 1963.

Potter, Henry C. *Reminiscences of Bishops and Archbishops.* New York, 1906.

Redpath, James. *A Guide to Hayti.* Boston, 1861.

Redkey, Edwin. *Black Exodus: Black Nationalist and Back-to-Africa Movements, 1890-1910.* New Haven, 1969.

Rotberg, Robert I. with Christopher C. Clague. *Haiti: The Politics of Squalor.* Boston, 1971.

Sandeen, Ernest R. *The Roots of Fundamentalism, British and American Millenarianism, 1800-1930.* Chicago, 1970.

Schorr, Joel. *Henry Highland Garnet.* Westport, 1975.

Shadd, Mary Ann. *A Plea for Emigration, or, Notes on Canada West in its Moral, Social, and Political Aspect.* Detroit, 1852.

Simpson, J. Montague. *Six Months in Port-au-Prince and My Experience.* Philadelphia, 1905.

Smith, John C. *The New Missionary Society.* New York, 1860

Smith, William E. *The Francis Blair Family in Politics.* New York, 1933.

St. John, Spenser. *Hayti; or the Black Republic.* London, 1884.

Staudenraus, P. J. *The African Colonization Movement, 1816-1865.* New York, 1961.

Stevens, William Bacon. *The Lambeth Conference of 1878, A Lecture.* Philadelphia, 1879.

Superintendent of Public Schools of the City of Buffalo. *Eighteenth Annual Report*. Buffalo, 1855.

Tyng, Charles R. *Life of Stephen H. Tyng*. New York, 1890.

Walters, Alexander. *My Life and My Work*. New York, 1917.

Warner, Robert. *New Haven Negroes, a Social History*. New Haven, 1961, ca. 1940.

Wyatt-Brown, Bertram. *Lewis Tappan and the Evangelical War Against Slavery*. Cleveland, 1969.

VII. Articles

Akpan, M. B. "Alexander Crummell and His African 'Race-Work': An Assessment of His Contributions in Liberia to African Redemption; 1853-1873," *Historical Magazine of the Protestant Episcopal Church* XLV (June 1976): 177-199.

Bell, Howard H. "Negro Nationality: a Factor in Emigration Projects, 1858-1861," *Journal of Negro History* XLVII (January 1962): 43-53.

"The Bishop of Haiti," *Quarterly Message Concerning Church Missions at Home* VI (October-December, 1898): 35-36.

Boyd, Willis D. "James Redpath and American Negro Colonization in Haiti, 1860-1862," *The Americas* XII (October 1955): 176-182.

Carter, Paul. "The Reformed Episcopal Schism of the Protestant Episcopal Church," *Historical Magazine of the Protestant Episcopal Church* XXXIII (September 1964): 225-238.

Coxe, Arthur C. "Visitation of the Mission in Haiti," *Spirit of Missions* XXXVIII (May 1873): 321-325.

Dean, David M. "The Domestic and Foreign Missionary Society Papers: Haiti: 1855-1939," *Historical Magazine of the Protestant Episcopal Church* XXXIX (March 1970): 94-95.

Geiss, Immanuel. "Notes on the Development of Pan-Afrikanism," *Journal of the Historical Society of Nigeria* III (June 1967): 719-740.

Giles, Etienne Victor. "James Theodore Holly, First Bishop of Haiti," *The Living Church* LXXI (February 28, 1925): 598.

Gross, Bella. "The First National Negro Convention," *Journal of Negro History* XXXI (October 1946): 435-443.

Hall, Charles B. "Mexico, Haiti and the Constitution," *The Church Review* XLIX (April 1887): 338–351.

Hancock, Harold B. "Mary Ann Shadd: Negro Editor, Educator and Lawyer," *Delaware History* XV (April 1973): 187–194.

Hayden, J. Carleton. "James Theodore Holly (1829–1911): First Afro-American Episcopal Bishop: His Legacy to Us Today," *Journal of Religious Thought* XXXIII (Spring-Summer 1976): 50–62.

Heinl, Nancy Gordon. "America's First Black Diplomat," *Foreign Service Journal* 50 (August 1973): 20–22.

Landon, Fred. "Henry Bibb, a Colonizer," *Journal of Negro History* V (October 1920): 437–447.

————. "Negro Migration to Canada after 1850," *Journal of Negro History* V (January 1920): 22–36.

McMaster, Richard K. "Henry Highland Garnet and the African Civilization Society," *Journal of Presbyterian History* XXXVIII (Summer 1970): 95–112.

Moses, Wilson J. "Civilizing Missionary: A Study of Alexander Crummell," *Journal of Negro History* LX (April 1975): 229–251.

Murray, Alexander L. "The Provincial Freeman: a New Source for the History of the Negro in Canada and the United States," *Journal of Negro History* XLIV (April 1959): 123–135.

Padgett, James A. "Diplomats to Haiti and Their Diplomacy," *Journal of Negro History* XXV (July 1940): 265–330.

Provine, Dorothy. "The Economic Position of the Free Black in the District of Columbia, 1800–1860," *Journal of Negro History* LVIII (January 1973): 61–72.

Redpath, James. "Notes on a Visit to Hayti," New York *Tribune*, June 25, 1859.

Sherman, Joan R. "James Monroe Whitfield, Poet Emigrationist: a Voice of Protest and Despair," *Journal of Negro History* LVII (April 1972): 169–176.

"Special Haiti Number," *Forth* 122 (March 1957): 6–23.

VIII. Dissertations and Unpublished Monographs

Freeman, Rhoda G. "The Free Negro in New York City in the Era Before the Civil War." Ph.D. dissertation, Columbia University, 1966.

Hurley, James P. "Walking Tours of the Museum of the City of New York: Bedford of Bedford Stuyvesant." Copy in Long Island Historical Society.

Jackson, James O., III. "The Origins of Pan-African Nationalism: Afro-American and Haytian Relations, 1800–1863." Ph.D. dissertation, Northwestern University, 1976.

McGlotten, Mildred Louise. "Rev. George Freeman Bragg, a Negro Pioneer in Social Welfare." M.A. thesis, Howard University, 1948.

Moore, Joseph G. "A Study of the Episcopal Church in the Missionary District of Haiti." The Unit of Research and Field Study of the National Council of the Protestant Episcopal Church, 1956.

Walker, George. "The Afro-American in New York City, 1827–1860." Ph.D. dissertation, Columbia University, 1975.

Wipfler, William Louis. "The Establishment and Development of L'Eglise Orthodoxe Apostolique Hatienne." M.A. thesis, General Theological Seminary, 1955.

# Index

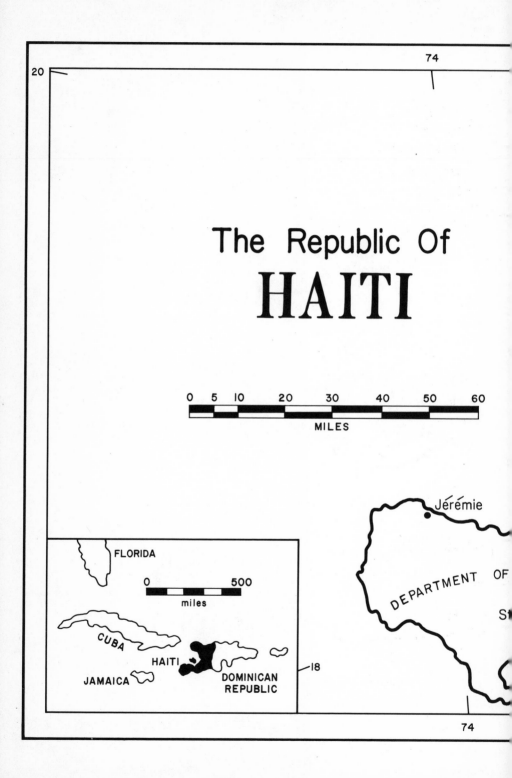

# The Republic Of
# HAITI

0 5 10 20 30 40 50 60

**MILES**

Jérémie

DEPARTMENT OF

S

FLORIDA

0       500

miles

CUBA

HAITI

JAMAICA

DOMINICAN
REPUBLIC

18

20

74

74